COMING HOME TO ME

Cassandra Tsolis

First edition 2024

Edited by Sierra Campbell – Editing By Sierra

Cover Design by Pnut

ISBN: 9798340172419

Contents

Introduction

I let my body be my bodyguard for a good majority of my life. At some point, my body decided it couldn't do that job anymore.

For so long, I didn't realize I kept myself safe by keeping men at a distance. My type of distance was more extreme than what I saw with those around me. It was more than the usual nervousness or anxiousness; it was extreme anxiety and panic. This distance was my shield of protection, but really, it was a stronghold of fear. I thought everything was normal until I started dating. That's when everything broke open. I was confused, but my body wasn't. It was acting as if it was under attack as if it needed safety. Meanwhile, my mind was playing catch up and trying to put the pieces together.

In my own research and journey, one statement that stood out to me was, "If you could have solved the problem already, you would have." For me, that was an indicator I needed more help. Professional help. Maybe that is why you are reading this book. Maybe you relate and want to know that you will be OK.

Step into my shoes. Maybe, as you walk with me through my journey, you will find the pieces you've been looking for in yours. We are all connected. We suffer and share joy together.

I welcome you into my process.

Part 1:
The Beginning

Acknowledging: The history & the behind the scenes

"There are wounds that never show on the body that are deeper and more hurtful than anything that bleeds." – Author Laurell K. Hamilton

The Initial Breaking — *Nothing Hidden Ministries Conference*

"Can I have a volunteer?" the conference speaker asks.

I sit, scanning the room as a middle-aged woman goes to the front of the stage. A group of strangers and I have spent the last three days working through layers of our pain and generational trauma with a group called Nothing Hidden Ministries. The main speaker for the day's topic, "Breaking Word Curses Over Our Lives," is interacting with the woman on stage. I notice she is not really looking him in the eye. She looks and then darts her gaze away quickly. I think, *I wonder what her experience has been like with men.*

The speaker probably notices her behavior, but he isn't thrown by it, and he gives her space to just *be.*

"Are you willing to walk through this exercise?" She nods in approval.

It starts with her closing her eyes as the speaker, now the facilitator, asks her to recite a word that is spoken over her.

"When I was a young adult, my dad called me a fucking whore, and a few months after, I ended up on a path that led to prostitution."

The facilitator, not moved, proceeds with, "Can you say out loud, 'I renounce the lie that I am a fucking whore?'"

She repeats the sentence timidly.

The facilitator gracefully says, "I invite you to say the full sentence as you heard it growing up."

Her chest wells up, and her eyes knit together as she takes a deep breath. Her body topples over immediately as she starts speaking. A well breaks within her. She weeps and releases the weight of that comment as the facilitator gives her space to feel. I sit there feeling the same release, and tears come from my own eyes. As the exercise continues, she experiences healing that washes out the memory and those painful words. I begin to question why I feel a connection to her story as if I am experiencing healing with her.

Sometimes the narratives of others' stories are part of the provision that comes into our lives. Their stories carry a part of our own story, and their release of healing opens us up to facing places in ourselves we may not fully be aware of yet. As I invite you into my story, my prayer, and my hope is that it holds pieces of your own. May you find healing, belonging, and peace knowing you are not alone in what you face and are overcoming.

Growing up, my grandmother frequently repeated this quote: "We may not have it all together, but together we have it all." May we open our eyes to our story and walk together through it all.

Uncovering Triggers — *Dance Movement Therapy Convention*

It is noon, and I am in a room full of adults. We are anticipating our next exercise at this movement-focused conference.

"Go around the room, stand in front of someone, and look them directly in the eyes for ten seconds," the instructor tells us.

OK. You got this, Cassie. You got this, I say to myself. *Not too awkward.*

As I walk around the room, I notice my body begin to stiffen. Next thing I know, my chest feels tight, and my body quickly starts to tense up. My body is yelling, *Girl! Get me out of here. Move faster!* Then, a strong sense of panic overcomes me as soon as I walk near a man I don't know.

I notice that I am unable to approach any man in the room comfortably, and my eyes fight any form of eye contact with a male. I continue the exercise while I try to dodge any man who comes in my direction.

What is wrong with me? I think. *Why can't I be normal?*

Are we willing to listen to our body when it has a story it wants to tell us?

Childhood and Environment

I thought my childhood was like everyone else's, even though I didn't really remember much of it. As I got older and visited home, my mom would share a memory, look at me, and say, "You don't remember that, do you?" It started to become a running joke between us.

Then, I started to wonder if I had memory loss or if something was wrong with me. I could only remember a few memories from my childhood. "That's what they call the overwhelmed mind," a counselor once told me. The current situation is too much to take in and is suppressed by the mind. Then, in the present, your mind is still carrying that weight.

Our minds have their own survival techniques; their own way to cope with what is being experienced. I started to question my past when my body had stronger reactions than my mind. I started to acknowledge the voice in my body when my mind felt blank. I knew something was there for such a long period of time that I thought what I was experiencing was normal fear. As my reactions in certain situations continued and even worsened, I knew there was something deeper to address.

Have you ever heard the song "Little Girl" by John Montgomery? The one where the children hid behind the couch as Jesus stood in the room, protecting them from their parents fighting? My early childhood had the same pattern; fighting, hiding, looped on repeat. This song was one I heard often. I could tell my mom found some type of peace in hearing it.

I was born to teenage parents, one with a strong Greek heritage. Just like in *My Big Fat Greek Wedding*, there was "Greek food, Greek babies, and Greek men." Their relationship was stifled from the start because it already broke two rules: my mom wasn't Greek, and my parents weren't married. Even though the "rules" may have been broken, my mom was not one to mess with. She made a way even if it was never made before. She was always like that—relentless.

Growing up, my dad was in the picture every other weekend while my mom took care of me full-time, and my stepfather came into the picture around the age of two. The scene started to change when a new baby was on the way. My life continued with a stepfather, stepbrothers, and a younger half-brother, while my real dad stayed present until my teenage years.

There are two other songs that mark my childhood. My mom still laughs when they are mentioned.

"A scrub is a guy that thinks he's fly and is also known as..." and you know the rest. The other song is "Gangsta's Paradise." Yes, this was our childhood. I'm sure this can give you an idea of the type of woman my mom was. She was grounded, real, and consistent. Even though I was around men growing up—my brothers, real dad, and stepfather—my mom was the only one who remained consistent.

The marriage between my stepfather and my mom was on and off for many years, so, to me, my mom became both parents. Somehow, she did it naturally.

Survival. My mom continued to be both parental figures when my biological father disappeared during my teenage years. I wouldn't realize until years later the impact that had on my life, the insecurities that took root within me, and the fear that began to grow subconsciously.

As the years went on, a separation from myself began to take place, and a foundation of fear began to take hold. I didn't realize how early it started. So my journey within—to find myself again—began to unfold.

Reflection

- As you heard parts of my childhood, did any memories of your own upbringing come to mind?

- What was your childhood environment like? Did you have both parents present? Were you an only child? Or did you have siblings or live with extended family?

- When you think of your childhood, what emotions—or lack thereof—come to the surface? How did that environment shape you?

Next Steps

- Take a moment to journal and reflect on the questions provided above. Write about any memories or emotions that arise.

Notes

- Sometimes the narratives of other peoples' stories are part of the provision that comes into our lives. Their stories carry a part of our own story, and their release of healing opens us up to facing places in ourselves we may not fully be aware of yet.

- Our minds have their own survival techniques and their own way of coping with what is being experienced.

Awareness: Opening our eyes to unresolved conflict reflected in our bodies

"The conflict between the will to deny horrible events and the will to proclaim them aloud is the central dialectic of psychological trauma." – Psychiatrist & Author Judith Herman

Triggered — *Dance Class Exercise*

I am scanning the room, looking for a way out. I panic as sweat starts to fill my shirt. "Find a partner," our teacher says as she starts pairing us up for dance class. This next exercise requires us to have half-body contact with another person. When I say half-body contact, I mean one person lays on the floor, and the other has to sit on them to create a visual effect. Mind you, she is pairing up individuals of the opposite sex. Not a big deal to others, but I'm slightly mortified.

As she is pointing out people to pair up, I quickly leave the class, pretending as if I am going to the restroom. I wait in the bathroom as long as I can before it becomes too obvious.

Cassie, tell her you don't feel comfortable with the exercise, I start debating with myself.

No! I can't do that. What will other people think? What if she thinks I am making this up?

All these thoughts start swarming my mind as my body goes numb.

Just like the story above, I lived through many similar moments thinking I was an anxious, awkward, insecure young adult. I started to identify with those feelings. Believing it was naturally who I was. It wasn't until memories like this one that I started to take note: something wasn't normal, and I needed to pay close attention.

There are many ways your body will signal to you that you need to listen. Those moments, I believe, are pivotal. As I share some of the stories from my journey, I hope it gives you insight into the ways your body might try to speak to you.

Escape or Confront — *Dance Workshop*

"Everyone, it's time to get into groups of two."

Another dance workshop; the focus: expanding our mobility and range. Immediately, I look around the room for a woman to partner with.

Cassie, if a man asks to partner with you, prepare to ask him to connect only in the safe touch zones, I rehearse in my head, preparing myself out of a sense of control and slight fear.

I see a man look in my direction, and I dart my gaze. I start to walk toward any woman I see.

That was a close one, I say to myself as the anxiety in my body spikes momentarily.

The teacher walks around the room to each one of us, slowly making her way to me.

"I see you hold a lot of tension in your body. You over-exaggerate and have a hard time letting go of control," she says to me.

Well, that's embarrassing. How can she see that through my movement?! I think to myself. *Did I make it that obvious?*

11

When I left that workshop, I continued hearing that comment like a broken record in my head. I realized that my body had exposed me. My movement and body language revealed there was unrest within myself. What I was experiencing internally—a loss of control—I was trying to gain externally through over-exaggerating to find a sense of stability.

Control was how I learned to stay safe, how I learned to create safety around me and within me, but there was more for me. More than this "control." A need for internal rest, internal security, and, primarily, internal healing.

Our bodies tell us a lot about where we are in life, what we've been carrying, and what we need to be free from. Movement exposes our default defense mechanisms and mediates the process of where we once lived to the new space we can walk into.

Release — *American College Dance Association Workshop*

I'm at a three-day dance conference, taking a variety of classes, and the title "Awareness of Spirit" caught my attention. I sign up for this class not knowing what to expect. As class starts, we all seem a little uncertain of what is next. The first exercise requires us to walk around the room and start to improv with a partner. It is a co-ed class, and every time I walk near a male, you know the pattern now, I either become stiff as a board or make a quick motion to move toward another partner who is a woman.

Why can't I just enjoy life, learn to connect with people, and not be so afraid?

Then comes exercise two. We are instructed to walk around the room and place our hand on a stranger's shoulder. While looking them in the eye, we are invited to think a good thought about them, sending the intention as an unspoken blessing.

OK, not too hard and not too bad, I mumble to myself.

Halfway through the exercise, I notice a middle-aged woman walking toward me. She comes up to me and looks me in the eye. A sense of comfort fills my body as I stand in front of her. She reaches out to put her hand on my shoulder, but I notice a slight change in demeanor as she decides to hug me instead. I hesitantly open my arms to engage with her, feeling slightly confused. Her warm smile meets my guarded energy.

Why is she looking at me like that? Do I look sad?

I let her in to hug me, thinking it will only be momentary. Moments pass by and she is still holding me. I attempt to keep my guard up as I notice a slight shift in my body. The tension begins to leave as I try to hold back the tears that start to rise. A force, a long-awaited arrival, meets my face with streams of release. The tears break out. Her hug melts the wall within me.

What is happening to me? I wonder to myself as this woman continues to hold me.

Another moment, I am taking note of my body speaking. But am I listening?

Our bodies hold stories; they are a container of memories. Sometimes we walk through life as our bodies hold their breath, waiting for someone safe to deeply exhale with. Just like that woman who held me, our bodies are waiting for comfort—for a space to be heard and acknowledged. It's easy to forget how much our bodies carry and how they walk us through.

When we affirm the feelings we experience in our bodies, we start to live in peace with ourselves instead of being at war. To find that peace, we have to start taking note of our feelings, reactions, and the ways our bodies are trying to communicate with us.

I started to take note that I couldn't look people in the eye—specifically men. Any close proximity freaked me out. I thought it was part of my personality at first—being shy, awkward, and anxious—but the more I thought about it, I realized it wasn't just that. I wouldn't just turn inward in certain situations—my body would go into shock and shut down. I had little understanding as to what was happening and why my reaction was that intense. It felt like I needed to solve a mystery, yet it was my body, so how could I do that?

You're probably thinking, '*It's obvious she experienced some form of abuse or sexual trauma.*' That is what I would think, too. However, for the first twenty-five years of my life, I didn't have any memory of abuse or sexual trauma. It wasn't until my body started to react in situations like these that I knew there was something deeper that I was holding onto.

From college on, I spent years in consistent therapy, talking about a single mother and an absent father, thinking that talk therapy was enough, but I began to question what else I needed.

Top-Down & Bottom-Up Therapy

In recent research, the first wave of therapy used with children who had experienced trauma in their environment was Cognitive Behavioral Therapy. This "top-down" approach addresses thinking patterns. Talk therapy was used to create new ways of thinking. However, this has shown that the somatic and biological aspects of the body still carry your trauma.

Body-based approaches (bottom-up), such as relaxation exercises, dance movement therapy, and yoga therapy, have shown more effectiveness when paired with Cognitive Behavioral Therapy. This research highlighted that talk therapy may not be enough to relieve the body of its experiences. However, these upcoming approaches that involve movement aided the body in releasing its trauma. (Goggin, Caitlyn. "The Efficacy of Dance/Movement Therapy for Trauma Affected Youth." *Lesley Univer-*

sity, 19 May 2018, https://digitalcommons.lesley.edu/expressive_theses/ 93/.)

"Talk therapy," also known as a top-down approach, addresses trauma from a cognitive standpoint. There are several aspects of your brain. The reptilian brain, or brainstem, is the oldest part of the brain and is in charge of automatic functioning. The limbic system, or the emotional brain, is responsible for your emotional experiences and regulation. The cortex, the youngest part of the brain, is in charge of your attention, memory, perception, and more.

"Imagine your brain is like a staircase, each step developed from the womb, and talk therapy addresses from the top step of the brain, but imagine starting from the bottom step." Walking up that staircase allows the impact of trauma to be addressed at its root. (Gregory, Amanda Ann. "How Bottom-Up Treatment Can Address Trauma. *Psychology Today*, 19 Dec. 2021, https://www.psychologytoday.com/us/blog/simplifying-c omplex-trauma/202112/how-bottom-treatment-can-address-trauma.)

For years I was aware of this fear and anxiety around men, yet the more I walked through my pain, I realized it's like trying to convince a toddler—the inner child within you—to not be afraid. I was aware on a cognitive level of the fear I held around men, the "top step" of the brain. However, I needed to heal from the starting point, the "bottom step," the source.

Confronted — *Nothing Hidden Ministries Conference*

"OK, everyone, it's time to move on to our next exercise. The next thirty minutes, we are going to practice what it would be like to go on dates," the conference speaker announces. The focus: learning to be a healthy individual, breaking generational patterns, and dealing with our "stuff" before dating.

Technically, speed dating.

I chuckle, thinking it's a joke, but as I look around, everyone else looks serious. So, what do you think I do? That's right! Without making eye contact, I try to casually leave the room. It is an instinctual response at this point—one I don't even think about. My body is like, "We out."

I stroll the hallway for a few minutes until I hear the next announcement. "We are actually going to discuss building healthy friendships and healthy relationships." My body sighs in relief. I know, from this point forward, if I ever want to pursue a relationship, I need to confront this fear and the root of it. Key phrase: *root of it.*

Fear. That was the main marker I didn't really have to take note of. It lived with me constantly. I started to partner with fear, thinking it was an indicator to not go in a certain direction. So with men, I would run, keep a distance, or know my strategies to keep me "safe." It's as if there were two people present at once within me. Part of me was aware of the fear, and another part of me, a default setting of survival, was operating, and it always told me to run.

You often hear "face your fears" or "do it afraid." Those phrases work when referring to the nervousness one feels when making a big decision or doing something out of their comfort zone. But this fear, my fear, around men was almost ingrained and instinctual.

I knew I was running from something, and for a good majority of my life, I thought I was doing the right thing by letting fear be my guide, my decision-maker—my sense of where *not* to go.

Awareness is the beginning. We can live a good amount of our lives by the perception of our past, not realizing how deeply our childhood experiences and environment have shaped our perspective of reality. As Bruce Lipton, an American Author of "Biology of Belief," shares, we use around 5% of our conscious brain, meaning when we are not focused on the present moment. The remaining 95% is controlled by our subconscious functioning. How we view the world and relate to people the way we do has clear indications from the environment we grew up in. Sometimes we can't remember our childhood environment—the trauma of past events can resurface decades later.

That described the first part of my twenties. I functioned out of a cognitive awareness of fear, yet my body was living from a subconscious condition, keeping men at an acquaintance level. I didn't realize how deep the pain in my body went until the latter half of my twenties when I let men into my life through dating and deeper friendships. In the right season and the right time, more memories, more answers, and more clarity began to surface.

What is left unresolved in our bodies will show up in other areas of life. That's the real journey—clearing out the trash and getting to live life fully and as whole as we can. Sometimes, our body will keep having the same reaction until we are ready to take note and listen. We can choose the pattern of default behavior because it has been our habit and form of defense, or we can walk through it, taking responsibility into our own hands to make new beliefs and ways of thought. All so we can be set free from what has kept our bodies captive.

Keys To Clarity — *Nothing Hidden Ministries Conference*

"May I ask you something?" My timid question rings as I approach the conference leader. "Throughout my journey and experiences, even while I've been here, I notice I hold a type of fear around men; however, I have few memories of something happening in my childhood."

She looks at me, waits for a moment, and says, "I would look at what you saw your mom experience growing up. Sometimes we learn behaviors from our parents and how they interacted with men or what they experienced with men. There could be something there."

Noted. Another piece for me to sit with, I think.

My mother's story held a lot of turmoil and pain but also an aroma of resilience. She experienced an upbringing of physical and verbal abuse, being in the presence of broken male figures that influenced a part of her childhood.

"Many of us unconsciously take on our parents' pain. As small children, we develop our sense of self gradually. Back then, we had not learned how to be separate from our parents and be connected to them at the same time. Perhaps we imagined that we could alleviate their unhappiness by fixing or sharing it. When we merge with a parent, we unconsciously share an aspect, often a negative aspect, of that parent's life experience. We repeat or relive certain situations or circumstances without making the very link that can set us free." (Wolynn, Mark. *It Didn't Start with You: How Inherited Family Trauma Shapes Who We Are and How to End the Cycle.* Penguin Books, 2017, pp 64.)

What we see as a child can also feel like our own experience. What is passed down from a previous generation can feel as if it is our own. I later learned that what I witnessed growing up, the hidden memories, and what was passed down in my bloodline would contribute to this stronghold of fear around men. Piece by piece we can all learn the story in our bodies.

Layer by layer and year by year, more will slowly come to the surface. We may not have all the details yet, but we don't always need to. When it's time, our bodies will share. Then we will know when it's time to listen and take action. This is the beginning of body awareness.

Reflection

Body awareness is how we begin to create space for our body's voice. Acknowledging where your body is holding tension, pain, or trauma is the start of saying, "Body, I am listening. What else would you like to tell me?" The next is getting the right help and letting that awareness lead you into finding a way to heal.

Take a minute. Did the stories I share resonate with you? Have you had a similar experience or reaction come up in your body?

Take a couple of minutes to journal those memories, moments, and thoughts. Being aware of our triggers helps us move toward the core of our wounding and shed light on the root of our trauma. As I continue to unravel my story, I will be sharing resources that have helped me process and reset my mind to walk out my healing effectively.

Next Steps: Awareness, Check. Releasing The Pain, The Next Step

Here are a few resources to help you step into mindfulness and continue the connection with yourself and your body.

Journaling Daily

For structure, I recommend:

- Artists Way – Julia Cameron – "Morning pages" – Writing down every thought, curiosity, idea—emptying your mind every morning in a journal before the day begins.

- Daily Examen (Created by St. Ignatius)

1. Become aware of God's presence.

2. Review the day with gratitude.

3. Pay attention to your emotions.

4. Choose one feature of the day and pray from it.

5. Look toward tomorrow.

- My personal examen (you can use this for reference)

  ○ Where did I see moments of peace/the Creator today?

  ○ Where did I miss the peace/Creator's presence?

  ○ What emotions came up for me today, and around what situations?

Breathwork/Mindfulness Applications & More
- Wim Hoff Method App

- The Pause App – John Eledridge – Guided Meditation (This one, in particular, is grounded in Jesus)

- Toogie App – Breath Work, Meditation, Movement & Community

- "The Gift of Triggers" – Adult Chair Podcast Natalie Grant (Spotify)

- Breath work – Online & in-person – Teresa Toogie Barcelo

- Breath work – Online & in-person – Elaine Wu (Being guided with breath to let your body show you where it's holding pain)

Bottom-Up Therapy (Further Reading & Information)
- EMDR – Eye Movement Desensitization and Reprocessing Therapy

  ○ https://www.psychologytoday.com/us/therapy-types/eye-mo

vement-desensitization-and-reprocessing-therapy

- Somatic Experiencing

  - https://www.psychologytoday.com/us/therapy-types/somatic-therapy

- Family Systems Therapy (Form of Psychotherapy)

  - https://www.psychologytoday.com/us/therapy-types/family-systems-therapy

- Expressive Arts Therapy

  - https://www.psychologytoday.com/us/therapy-types/expressive-arts-therapy

Notes

- Our bodies signal to us when they need our attention.

- The growing "bottom-down" approach to therapy has become more helpful when aided by Cognitive Behavioral Therapy in relieving the body of trauma through movement and breathing-based exercises.

- The triggers we continue to experience are pins in the roadmap of our healing story. Those patterns of reaction reveal that there is something deeper underneath for us to pay attention to.

- Awareness is introducing yourself to your body's voice. It is the beginning of a beautiful partnership that your body has been waiting for.

Undoing: What relationships uncover

"In order to change, people need to become aware of their sensations and the way that their bodies interact with the world around them. Physical self-awareness is the first step in releasing the tyranny of the past." — Bessel A. van der Kolk, The Body Keeps the Score: Brain, Mind, and Body in the Healing of Trauma

"The lid of the jar is coming off." I'm listening attentively as my counselor begins to explain. "All the suppressed 'stuff' is getting washed out," she continues. The imagery evokes a worrisome response in me, thinking, *Is this all going to come out at once? What does that look like?* This wasn't going to be the last time I heard that phrase.

In the 'right' or unpredicted time, suppressed memories and wounds can begin to surface. For me, the journey of unraveling started here: dating. I wish it was a one-and-done thing, but like most things, it's a process.

Body Language — *Coffee Date*

At a local coffee shop, the guy I am interested in is waiting in line with me. It's one of our first dates. We order, grab our drinks, and sit down. I can smell the aroma of coffee, hear the chatter of people around us, and feel the warmth of the sun coming in through the window. Without much hesitation, we jump into conversation as we sip our drinks.

"Are you OK?" I heard him say at one point. I am anxiously playing with a ring on my finger as part of my body starts shaking.

What is wrong with me? Why am I shaking?

With a few words, I begin to describe how I am feeling, and without hesitation, my date begins to pray for me. Little did I know, this was the beginning—the beginning of a long road of cleaning out the history of my past, an abandonment wound, and the generational pain my body held on to.

"Traumatic symptoms are not caused by the 'triggering' event itself. They stem from the frozen residue of energy that has not been resolved or discharged; this residue remains trapped in the nervous system, where it can wreak havoc on our bodies and spirits. The long-term, alarming, de-bilitating, and often bizarre symptoms of PTSD develop when we cannot complete the process of moving in, through, and out of the 'immobility' or 'freezing' state." (Levine, Peter. *Waking the Tiger*, North Atlantic Books 1997.)

The shaking was my first precursor to the beginning of signals that my body would begin to expose. I would slowly come to understand that the shaking—the reactions—all were ways my body was trying to release the energy from the overwhelming past experiences that still remained.

Filling In The Gaps — *Family Conversation*

"Mom, can I ask you something?" I murmur as I start rubbing my hands out of some sense of normalcy. I really didn't want to ask this question, but I know I need to. It's heavy, and it feels out of the blue, but at this point, it's worth it.

"Did something ever happen to you or me when I was younger? I mean—abuse, rape, or something along those lines? I'm asking because I've noticed that when I hang out around men or go on dates, my body starts shaking."

My mom sits there quietly before she begins to answer. She starts to tell me this memory that I have no recollection of. "You were about two years old. As you were sitting in the backseat of our car, I heard you ask, 'Mom, does it hurt when he hits you?'"

I take a moment as I hear her question repeat in my head. "Does it hurt when he hits you?" Trying to see if I can remember that memory and that scene from my childhood, I slowly take in what feels like new information.

This goes along with what the conference leader from Nothing Hidden Ministries shared. "*Sometimes we learn behaviors from our parents and how they interacted with men or what they experienced with men. There could be something there,*" I remind myself. A key memory was uncovered. A stepping stone in the right direction of understanding what my body was holding. Even though the abuse wasn't directed toward me, it would be something I internalized, something my body would carry, and the beginning stage of building my narrative around men. As I continued on in my journey, I learned that there was more to my story. This started to bring clarity as I continued unraveling the memories my body was physically signaling to me.

I started to scratch the surface of my pain when I began dating seriously. After that first date at the coffee shop, I started dating this guy (let's call him Rey) for almost two years. Within those two years, I saw myself develop into a person I would have never imagined. I transitioned into living in a sense of constant worry, overthinking, and complete internal chaos.

"People often unconsciously choose a mate who will trigger their wounds. In this way, they have an opportunity to see, own, and heal the painful and reactive parts of themselves. Like the perfect mirror, the chosen partner reflects what sits unclaimed and unfinished at the core of the other." (Wolynn, Mark. *It Didn't Start with You: How Inherited Family Trauma Shapes Who We Are and How to End the Cycle*. Penguin Books, 2017.)

The Death Threats — *Dinner With Friends*

"I will meet you there," I say to Rey as we drive to meet our friends for dinner. I am feeling a little unsettled from an ongoing discussion—more like conflict—Rey and I are having. I try to put it aside as we get ready to go out to eat. We are meeting our friends for dinner, and I'm trying to pull my thoughts and self together. I pull into the parking lot, head inside, and meet our friends at the table.

"What are you thinking of getting?" Rey asks me as we look over the menu. My mind is juggling multiple thoughts. *Do I feel hungry? How do I put aside our last conversation?* Then, something strikes me. My eyes focus on the table in front of me, reaching for stability as my surroundings go silent. Time freezes, and everything stops as I hear a voice say, "You are going to die."

I look up from the table, shocked I zone out for a moment, wondering if I was the only person who heard it and if I heard it correctly. A war of thoughts takes place in my mind as I try to act casually somehow. Before I can pull myself out of the cloud of dread that starts to sweep over me, I hear a hopeful whisper say, "Cassie, it's just the beginning."

I am going to be real here because maybe you need to hear it, too. As my relationship with Rey continued, I developed an anxiety disorder. Obsessive thoughts, constant worry, weight loss, loss of appetite, lack of sleep. I started to hear thoughts like, *You are going to die*, often, either while I was alone or in groups. I was living in a constant state of fear.

This relationship began to mirror how suppressed and deep the trauma in my body was. The closer I got to intimacy, the more I saw how little my body trusted men, if at all. The reactions of my body, in addition to the barrage of thoughts, made me feel "out of control." I grasped for any sense of stability by trying to control my environment, my partner, and my circumstances.

I was looking for control outside of myself when I really needed it internally. I felt anxiously attached to my partner but I knew my attachment was disorganized; at times avoidant and other times anxiously in need. Wanting to be close, then pushing my partner away. I was deep in denial, not realizing the depth of my pain and what my body was unraveling. Even though I had an awareness of the trauma from my past, I couldn't fully understand why my body was responding the way it was.

Before meeting Rey, I wasn't in any serious relationships. If anything, they lasted a month or two because I would be so overcome with fear I couldn't engage well. Looking back, my relationship with my dad played a role in how I related to men. My dad and I were considered close growing up—he was a real friend and emotionally present. With life circumstances, as I got older, he disappeared. It was about fourteen years before I would see him again. That abandonment was conscious in my mind. However, my body held it differently, and it showed up the closer I got to men.

The Dialogue — *Leaving A Lunch Meeting*

I was leaving a restaurant after having lunch with a few family friends. As we were leaving, I was halted by a question.

"Cassie, are you OK? You don't look so good," a woman from the group asked. I started to figure out what I wanted to say while all eyes turned toward me. I started feeling a bit cornered, and my self-conscious thoughts heightened.

"I am doing OK," I replied, but she didn't stop there.

"No, Cassie. You do not look OK. I am concerned." She looked at me as if she was about to cry. I sensed her intention of empathy as a flood of shame, embarrassment, and numbness cloaked over me.

I nodded my head, not knowing how to respond, as everyone stared at me. I quickly turned to walk to my car as the tears unraveled on my face.

"I have never dealt with this before. The anxiety, the worry, the loss of appetite. Why is this coming up now? Will I have to deal with this forever?" My questions erupted out of frustration. "I never asked for this, and I feel shame for something I didn't choose." All these thoughts and emotions came with the onset of anxiety.

These symptoms kept up as I continued my relationship with Rey. Dating was cutting at the core of my wounds that I didn't know how to attend to. My connection to myself started to feel foreign. As if I didn't know who I really was under all the emotional and mental chaos.

What felt so foreign at the time, I later learned, was so common. They say the subconscious mind holds what it experienced when we were young. Even though we are in a new situation and around new people, the subconscious still operates out of its reality, which is our past.

So, what can I do next?

Taking Thoughts Captive — *Relationship Counsel*

"Cassie, it's like a love and hate relationship with intimacy when we live from places of trauma," Rey and I's mentors began to share. "That's when the shift happens—being aware of how we have been living from a wound versus a healthier version of ourselves."

Back to my relationship with Rey. As we sit at our mentor's house the whole evening, I keep hearing, "For our struggle is not with flesh and blood but with principalities, rulers and the power of darkness," (Ephesians 6:12) and "It is time, Cassie, to take your thoughts captive," (2 Corinthians 10:5). I remember reading those scriptures and telling God, "I cannot even tell you what thoughts I am having. My body is simply reacting."

I quickly began to understand the discipline of taking notes of these thoughts. Thoughts that ranged from, *He is going to leave you. He doesn't really care. He's forgotten about you.* The tool is recognizing these thoughts, surrendering them in the moment—which I did multiple times a day or hour—and choosing the opposite perspective. For example, changing, *He doesn't care* to *Maybe he is busy right now and doesn't have the capacity to reach out.*

I had a choice to learn to listen to a negative tape that spoke from an abandonment wound or start carving out a new pathway of thought with the continual practice of surrender and an opposing perspective to challenge my automatic response.

Little did I know then, those wounds from my past—layers of unforgiveness and unspoken trauma—were an open door to my uncontrolled thoughts. Where there isn't love, there is fear, and out of fear, we control, manipulate, and act in ways not normal to our nature. We act as if we are living to survive.

From that evening, I knew it would be a continuous process, a painful yet beautiful journey to let love into those wounds I had carried for so long.

Finding Clarity — *Dance Movement Therapy Convention*

Here I am in a room full of women, uncertain of what to expect. I came to Florida to be a part of a Dance Movement Therapy Conference, hoping to find direction for the next steps of my life. The first seminar is "Incorporating Evidence-Based Practices into Dance Movement Therapy with Eating Disorder Patients."

As I sit, I notice I am in a room of counselors, clinicians, and graduate students. An hour into the seminar, as I started to feel like everyone there was talking about patients with eating disorders, I wondered if what I was experiencing would be classified as such. I personally am looking for healing. As we embody different practices, one speaker catches my attention when I hear her say, "It is common to see eating disorders and anxiety disorders arise in romantic relationships."

Near the end of our time, I decide to walk up to the speaker and ask a personal question. Her answer came as a surprise. "In safe, romantic relationships, the nervous system feels secure enough to start addressing what has been suppressed for so long." Immediately, a wave of emotion comes out of me.

"So, you're telling me something isn't wrong with me? This is normal?" I ask.

"Yes, it is very common," she replies.

Cassie, hold it together, hold it together, I try saying to myself as a wave of relief washes over me. The tears unfold on my face without invitation as I let her words replay in my mind, *"Yes, it is very common."*

I needed to hear I wasn't crazy. I needed to know I was going to be OK. A piece of my healing was solidified that day as I walked away knowing that what I was facing was not foreign. It was so common.

The Brain — *Understanding Research*

This was my training ground: romantic relationships. Learning to be aware of my thoughts and triggers and disassemble them with a new narrative of truth. These relationships became my ultimate mirror, showing me parts of myself I wasn't fully aware of. Ultimately, it taught me to face my pain, face myself, and mature in taking responsibility for my healing. As I continued to research and study, I learned how influential our upbringing is on our brain and how that plays a role in how we relate to the world and how we function, especially in dating.

Understanding scientifically what is happening in the brain helps us understand what is being triggered in the body. The amygdala is a part of our brain that is responsible for detecting threats and possible dangers. The right part of our brain, also known as the emotional side, starts developing in the womb, while the left side of our brain, the logical side, starts to develop after we are born. Sometimes before we are able to process and acknowledge what threat is actually occurring, information reaches our right brain first, in which case our body can already be responding.

This spoke volumes to me. For so long, I had moments where my body would start shaking, and I'd feel nauseated or panicked without knowing what was happening. I could hear the comments I've heard from many videos and books saying, "Change your thoughts." I wanted to scream, "What thoughts?!"

Understanding the amygdala, depending on personal experiences and trauma, we can see a present moment from a past lens. Our body has now created a default setting with our response to possible danger. Changing thoughts and talking it out may not be enough. While a bottom-up therapy approach can assist in effectiveness, what's needed is to let the body release what it's carrying.

Essentially, in dating, my body was living in the past while I was still in the present. I was invited into the journey of releasing what my body was holding and being given the gift of living in the present moment. After that relationship, which ended shortly after that conversation at our mentor's house, I left everything to start a new chapter. I transitioned out of non-profit work that I had been a part of for four years, left a community I had been living in for about seven, and left my relationship with Rey.

My new season started in Los Angeles, where I would revive my soul and pursue an artistic endeavor I put on the back burner for so long. I didn't know then, but the more layers I walked through in my healing, the worse it would get before it could get better. The moment I became aware it was my pain to address and acknowledged what I needed to face and take responsibility for, it all got worse. The pain unleashed. I knew the other side was coming but it felt far.

As we journey in our healing, we take back our ground—the security in our bodies and our lives—back from the fear and pain that paralyzed us for so long. That is the real work of letting God move within, letting the truth resurrect the broken parts of us so they can be used for good, and discontinuing a legacy of brokenness. The other side is coming. You can make it through. If you feel like it is getting worse for you, let me tell you; that is a sign it could be getting better.

Reflection

- What is coming up for you as you hear this part of my story? Are parts of my story connecting to your own?

- In what ways have you built a deeper understanding of your body through being in intimate relationships?

- Do you notice any symptoms that arise in your romantic relationships?

- Have you noticed anything new coming up in your body in your own dating process?

Additional Exercise

To preface, I found a lot of clarity and understanding when reading ancient stories of individuals. This one, in particular, was of a man who had been ill for thirty-plus years. At that time, people who were labeled ill or had birth abnormalities were alienated to a certain area. This area had a pool that was believed to bring healing to any person who touched it first after an angel appeared, which happened once a year.

However, this man was lying on a mat. He couldn't walk or reach the pool and completely gave up before he had an interaction with Jesus. I invite you, if you feel open to reading the story, to see what stands out to you. A guided way of reading this story is provided below.

Gospel contemplation, also known as Ignatian contemplation, is an imaginative prayer through scripture. This prayer technique is a way of deeply engaging with scripture through imaginative interaction. One places themselves in a story to sense the surroundings and presence of the scene.

Take twenty to twenty-five minutes to fully engage in this next exercise. Open up the story in John 5:1-9 (NLT Version). I encourage you to read it aloud five times. Walk yourself through these questions, and after reading it once, ask yourself question number one, and after reading it twice, ask yourself question number two, and so forth.

- Where am I in this story? Am I the man lying down, am I in the crowd, or am I far away?

- What do I see, hear, or sense in the story?

- How is Jesus interacting with me in this story?

- Is there anything I want to say to Jesus? Is there anything Jesus is saying to me?

- What is the invitation for me?

I encourage you to take some time to journal what is coming up for you. Throughout the week, be open to how the Creator will continue to speak to you through this image and story.

Next Steps

If you resonate with any part of these mini-stories, the next step for you could be one of these options: mind-body-based classes, counseling, specialized therapy, or support groups. It is good to read, research, and consult with friends or individuals who have similar experiences. I would also highly recommend seeking professional help in addition to your own self-work. To go along with seeking professional help, it doesn't hurt to try movement-based classes, exercises, and techniques that help bring a deeper connection with you and your body.

Notes

- In the right time, more memories and wounds will surface. The body knows when it is safe to release.

- Relationships are our ultimate mirror; showing us more of ourselves that we didn't know was there.

- The right brain, the emotional brain, starts developing in the womb, while the left brain starts developing after we are born. When we experience trauma, the left brain receives information later than the right brain, meaning we react before we logically understand if there is a threat or not.

- Our bodies can react from memory (the subconscious) because the present situation feels familiar to the past.

- God wants to partner with us to heal, rewire, and live fully in the present without the residue of our past pain.

Resources

- ADTA — American Dance Therapy Association: https://www.adta.org/

  ○ Workshops that cover a variety of topics

- Self-Reclaimed: https://www.instagram.com/selfreclaimed/

  ○ Workshops, Dialogues, & Space to empower community against sexual assault & domestic violence

- Asian Mental Health Project: https://www.asianmentalhealthproject.com/

  ○ Dialogues, Collaborations, Events centered around education and mental health awareness

- https://www.instagram.com/asianmentalhealthproject/

- <u>Switch On Your Brain</u> — Dr. Caroline Leaf

- <u>Waking the Tiger</u> — Peter Levine

Releasing: Breaking open to heal

"The unconscious insists, repeats, and practically breaks down the door, to be heard." – Annie Rogers, The Unsayable

The Core — Phone Conversation

I t definitely gets worse before it gets better. It's 8 p.m. and I am driving to my grandmother's house as my body starts shaking.

OK, breathe, Cassie. Breathe.

I look down and notice I have an incoming call from a friend I haven't spoken to in a while. I answer the phone out of curiosity.

"Cassie, a mutual friend of mine, told me to reach out to you and said my story with men might be helpful," she shares.

"What a perfect time to call because I have no idea what's happening to me," I begin. "It all started about a month ago when I started dating again. But this last encounter scared me. I was driving to meet someone for dinner, and I already wasn't feeling well from the morning. I woke up immediately feeling nauseous in the morning and was doing my best to calm myself down. Halfway there, while I was in the car, I noticed a blanket of anxiety start to come over me. It's like the closer I got to the destination of the date, something started to shift. It felt hard to breathe, and nausea began to kick in."

"This all sounds familiar, Cassie, but keep going," she reassures me.

"I started deep breathing, speaking affirmations, but nothing was help-ing until I, without thinking, threw up. I was shocked and scared because that had never happened before. I didn't know what was happening to my body," I continue. "Now my body is constantly shaking, and I don't know how I got here or what to do next." As I share what I am experiencing, little did I know, "it gets worse before it gets better" would play out over the next four to six months for me.

"Cassie, what your body is experiencing is everything I have experienced before," she reassures me. She starts to share her experience in dating, which is not identical to mine, but similar.. She goes on to tell me, "When I was going on dates, my stomach would feel full, at times queasy, and at some points, I would even throw up. It got to the point that, every three weeks, I would be throwing up for the whole week. All day, with little food, trying to even take in water was a challenge. Doctors couldn't find anything wrong, yet a psychologist began to ask if I was stressed. That was where my journey began. I learned this was my subconscious functioning from past memories that kept my body imprisoned to that way of living," she shared.

She went on to explain, "Past memories had taught me that men were dangerous, and situations that slowly invited intimacy became a trigger and threat to my system. My unconscious mind kicked in when I started to feel out of control; it was trying to find a sense of security again."

All I want to know is how I make it stop, and how I move past the shaking, I think.

I've dealt with what felt like the worst in dating already, yet here I am, facing another layer that felt harder than ever before.

The way our body speaks can come in many forms. Through those forms, it's our body's attempt to ask for our attention. "When we try to resist feeling something painful, we often protract the very pain we're trying to avoid. There is something about the action of searching that blocks us from what we seek. Something valuable can be going on inside of us, but if we're not tuning in, we can miss it." (Wolynn, Mark. *It Didn't*

Start with You: How Inherited Family Trauma Shapes Who We Are and How to End the Cycle. Penguin Books, 2017.)

Will we tune in? Tune into the emotions, behaviors, and experiences coming to the surface? Are we willing to be taken there?

Home — *The Climax* — *Lazarus Season*

My eyes peel open as I awaken to another day. I'm lying on the guest bed of my mother's house as I notice something. My heart starts racing, my arms start shaking, and I'm gasping for breath as my body begins to surrender to the adrenaline rushing through me. I'm on high alert, yet I feel I have no control over my body. I peel myself off the bed in hopes to get up and grab food. My body goes numb as my mind swarms with endless thoughts. The surrounding hallway becomes a blur as my legs carry me to the kitchen. I reach for an apple and walk outside, trying to distract my mind from the symptoms as I meet the breath of fresh air touching my body.

I hope this is momentary. I don't know what is happening, and I'm scared, I whisper to myself as my eyes start to water.

I had spent the last couple of months jumping back into dating while uncovering deeper wounds. The unraveling began a few days before that phone call. That night, as I talked with my friend, little did I know what I was about to walk through. It all came, and it felt like all at once. The climax of my body's reactions started here when I returned home—to my mother's home—for a visit.

I was with my family when I started to notice frequent and constant panic attacks. Daily and then almost hourly. Thoughts were racing through my mind.

What is happening to my body?

Please, no more.

Will I ever be over this?

Can't I just be normal?

I didn't know what was happening—my body seemed to react first, with my thoughts coming second.

"If we are brave enough to go beneath the thoughts, go beneath the behaviors, and seek out the pain in our bodies, our bodies will lead us to healing. Our bodies will lead us to the core wound, and the core wound will inform our minds," said Shauna Quigley in one of her TED Talks.

I was at that point. My body was taking over. I had to start the journey of letting my body lead me into healing over letting my mind dictate what I needed to do. It's slightly terrifying when you have lived a certain way for so long, and now your body is demanding you to stop. These are the moments that show you how much your body has done for you, how much it has carried, how much it has sacrificed for you, and really how much it wants you to listen.

I immediately reached out for help. Spoke to counselors, doctors, and my friend, as I let my body lead me to the core wound. At times, it didn't feel like it was going to end or heal, but I had to let my body lead me, putting my trust in it first. The wholeness I needed and desired could only come through having a different leader, and for the first time, I said "yes" to my body.

Run or Go Through — *Blood Test Appointment*

"Get in the car, I'll drive." My friend picks me up for my blood work appointment. I am trying to still function with little to no appetite, my body quivering, and my mind in a downward spiral. It is day seven of frequent panic attacks, and I feel as if I am losing my mind—or trying to find it.

"Cassie, I want to tell you a dream a friend once told me."

Please be encouraging. Tell me how this is going to end, I think.

"In the dream, someone is sinking in quicksand and they are waiting for someone to lift them up, but instead, the person who came to help them didn't pull them up. They pushed them through." Sitting there, I am slightly encouraged and slightly terrified. "Sometimes our healing comes when we go through it," my friend says to me.

How much more do I have to go through to be whole? Is this just the beginning or the end? Am I going to even make it through? The cynicism in my head questions.

The next few months involved confronting unimaginable fear. I tried to manage my anxiety, tried to control the constant nausea, and tried to feel like I was in control of my thoughts. It was a level I had never experienced before. I would wake up either shaking or caught in a whirlwind of thoughts as my body started to tense up.

My friend, who called me that night, spent two months walking with me daily, helping me listen to my body and comforting myself. In the meantime, I spoke to my counselor, had inner-healing sessions, and continued to connect with people who I knew had walked through this anxiety. It was through the words of others and the companionship of my friend that gave me hope that I, too, could face this.

The fear I had to face manifested for me through my stomach. It had always been that way since childhood. I missed out on school and spent days in bed, all due to chronic stress that resulted in consistent stomach issues. Through years and years of underlying stress, the symptoms got worse when triggered, which in my case, was around men.

The nausea is where we can hold fear. The longer it is suppressed, the more physical symptoms may arise. There is fear wrapped around what we know and don't know and what is passed down to us. The uncertainty with our own bodies can make us feel like a stranger in our own skin.

"Once you start approaching your body out of curiosity rather than fear, everything shifts." (Van der Kolk, Bessel. *The Body Keeps the Score: Brain, Mind, and Body in the Healing of Trauma*. Penguin Books, 2014.) In those seasons, where we are confronting the core of our pain, there are stories and people who are our divine provision. Their stories hold a light to what feels dark within us. Not only are there people who come alongside us to walk us through, but there are also two other highly needed tools. One is our body, listening instead of fearfully pushing back, and two, the Holy Spirit—the advocate—to walk with us.

Pushing Past The Panic — *Evening At Home — Lazarus Season*

"I feel like eating a salad," I say to myself, while in the same breath thinking, *But I have hardly eaten all day.* I am afraid to even attempt to eat because, even at the sight of food, my body starts trembling.

It's week two after being back from my family's home when all this started, and it's a few days after my blood test. I decide to listen to what I am feeling and eat a salad. Twenty minutes in, I recognize the shaking, the swarming thoughts, and the fear is gone. It's a brief vacation from the external chaos. My body can breathe and I can think clearly.

From that little instance, I decide to start listening more closely to what my body wants to eat. I knew symptoms were arising physically from long-term suppression of fear and trauma. Not only did I need emotional counsel, I needed to seek medical help. I decided I couldn't lead this process—I had to surrender, and I had to listen.

In this intense season, in saying "yes" to my body and surrendering to God what healing would look like, walking through it felt very unconventional and radical. In the midst of what felt like hell, uprooting memories, and full-blown anxiety, I felt an invitation from God to have fun.

I thought, *How can I have fun right now? What does that even look like?*

That, however, was what I needed.

Don't Think, Just Drive — *Evening At The Beach* — *Lazarus Season*

I am driving home, and I hear a thought while feeling this nudge to go do something.

Drive to the beach.

I'm thinking, *It's late. Am I hearing that right?*

However, I chose to just go. About forty minutes later, there I am, sitting on the beach, watching the waves crash as the stars hang in the sky like a stationary mobile. I start talking to God and listening as if someone is next to me.

Is this really worth it? part of me is questioning and the other part of me is thinking, *Breathe and take a minute to be present.*

Within thirty minutes, I begin to feel something in my stomach. A small wave of hunger begins to grow. A miracle!

I am not sure how long this hunger will last, so let's eat while I can, I say in my head with excitement while I rush to my car.

It was in these little daily invitations, like "go on a walk, go outside, go do something," that I found a form of healing. I surrendered to taking life and my health a day at a time as I waited and was attentive to any invitation or nudge I'd get to go do something. What I thought was just being obedient to God was actually an invitation to find my home again back in my body. Coming back home to me.

I was being a friend to my body and reconciling the toxins that had divorced us for so long. God knew what I needed, and in surrendering to the process, I let the Creator lead me back to myself.

Along with having fun, I intentionally listened to my body while consulting doctors, family, and friends—in addition to reading books. After those few months, I started to regain the strength I felt I had completely lost. With more dedication, I started to do more research and dive in with grace toward my body and myself.

The journey now is committing to walking through. You may be thinking, *Well, how do I do that?* The questions I encourage us to ask ourselves are: What is our body feeling? Is this physical, mental, emotional, or spiritual? What kind of help do we need moving forward in these different areas?

Our healing will require solitude and our healing will require community. Be aware of who comes into your life, because, in the right timing, there will be unexpected people who help carry us through parts of our story. Those are the people who helped me experience a piece of restoration, provision, and a part of the heart of God.

Reflection

Take 20 to 25 minutes to fully engage in this next exercise. Open up the story of the woman mentioned here in Luke 8:43-48 (NLT Version). For context, this woman had an issue of blood for twelve years and was considered an outsider in the community. The fact that she was bleeding made her "unclean" socially. She had seen doctors and spent all her money to try and get well. Even though she was labeled by her community a certain way, when she heard of the teacher coming, she took the risk publicly and took action for her healing.

I encourage you to read it aloud multiple times. Walk yourself through these questions as you read through.

- Where am I in this story? Am I the woman, am I in the crowd, or am I close or far away from Jesus?

- What do I see, hear, or sense in the story?

- How is Jesus interacting with me in this story?

- Is there anything I want to say to Jesus? Is there anything Jesus is saying to me?

- What is the invitation for me?

I encourage you to take some time to journal what is coming up for you. Throughout the week, be open to how the Creator will continue to speak to you through this image and story.

Next Steps

This is a great space to journal if anything is coming up for you as I am sharing more intimate parts of my journey. With great vulnerability comes great power. I heard a speaker once say, "The pain in me becomes the power in me." We are in the process of turning our pain into power and turning what was meant to destroy us into weapons of our own liberation.

Notes

- "If we are brave enough to go beneath the thoughts, go beneath the behaviors, and seek out the pain in our bodies, our bodies will lead us to healing. Our bodies will lead us to the core wound, and the core wound will inform our minds." – Shauna Quigley

- We experience healing in layers. Then there are seasons where we face our pain at its core. When the core of our wounds hit the surface, our bodies somehow know it is the right time.

- In the body, the stomach is where we hold fear. The longer we suppress it, the more physical symptoms may arise.

- Sometimes we can no longer lead the process—we have to surrender and listen.

- In those seasons, where we are confronting the core of our pain, there are stories and people who are our divine provision. Their stories hold a light to what feels dark within us.

- Be aware of who comes into your life, because, in the right timing, there will be unexpected people who help carry us through parts of our story. Those are the people who I experience a piece of restoration, provision, and a part of the heart of God in.

Mind-Body Resources

- Wim Hoff Breathing Techniques – "Tumo Breathing" https://www.wimhofmethod.com/breathing-exercises

- Sadghuru & Breathing Techniques – https://isha.sadhguru.org/us/en

  - This website offers free webinars on yoga, meditation, and breathing techniques. I took a few classes and applied what I felt suited me or what I felt needed to be added to my mornings. It's worth trying to see what ways our body can communicate to us through breath and movement.

- Jason Valloton – Video Series – Anxiety & Healing Wounds

  - https://www.youtube.com/results?search_query=overcoming+anxiety+jason+vallotton

Book Recommendations
- *Panic to Power* – Lucinda Bassett

- *Breath* – James Nestor (Extensive research & techniques used to heal the body through breath)

Symptoms: Listening to the pain

"The body never lies." – Martha Graham

As we journey in connecting to ourselves, we take inventory of how well we are listening to our bodies. The body has a way of speaking, physically showing us where we're at internally. If we are experiencing disease in our lives and in our bodies, from my own story, I know our bodies will show physical symptoms of disease.

Road-mapping — *Connecting the Dots*

I started noticing a connection in regard to upbringing and health in the stories of the women I read articles about. "I had my daughter when I was nineteen, and I was a single mom for quite some time," a temporary co-worker once shared with me. "I am now on thyroid medication because my thyroid gave out at a young age."

This narrative was one of many I started to hear, and this one, in particular, matched my mother's. Paralleling the story of my mother, I came across another woman who described an upbringing of abuse and neglect and was later diagnosed with thyroid cancer. I began to see this thread; a common theme. A narrative around upbringing, genes, and thyroid symptoms. I also heard about stomach cancer, nausea, ulcers, and stomach complications. All pointing back to the digestive function of the body, which, I knew all too well, resembled my family line as well.

"Scientists have discovered that chromosomal DNA – the DNA responsible for transmitting physical traits, such as the color of our hair, eyes, and skin – surprisingly makes up less than 2 percent of our total DNA. The other 98 percent consists of what is called noncoding DNA (ncDNA), and is responsible for many of the emotional, behavioral, and personality traits we inherit." (Wolynn, Mark. *It Didn't Start with You: How Inherited Family Trauma Shapes Who We Are and How to End the Cycle.* Penguin Books, 2017.)

My questions started to be: How does trauma show itself in our physical bodies, and what is trauma's role in the onset of auto-immune disorders, especially affecting the thyroid? What is our body physically showing us about the inner workings of our mental and emotional health?

Foreshadowing — *Where the Symptoms Really Started — Community College Staff Training*

I am at a weekend community college staff training surrounded by thirty to forty colleagues. We have two days of team building, bonding, and vision casting for the upcoming school year. It is the middle of day one and this story catches my attention.

"There was a staff worker who started her journey on staff exuberant and excited. She was passionate, devoted, and loved her work. However, about three years in, she started to experience signs of burnout, and her health was declining. After leaving staff work, she had a season where she stayed in bed for almost three months straight." Shocked and slightly alarmed by the story, I silently make a vow to never get to that point.

Little did I know, leaving that staff training, that three years later, almost exactly, I would be just like her. Leaving staff and moving to L.A., where I spent the next three months in and out of bed, contending for my healing and asking for refreshment for my soul. I took a big step. I left a community of seven years, a relationship of two years, and a job of four years to move somewhere new.

I came to L.A. for three months to be a part of a dance training program, thinking it would only be temporary. In those three months, I didn't have much self-awareness of what I was going through. However, I knew my body was showing physical symptoms of where my body, soul, and mind were at. My symptoms included oversleeping, exhaustion, little energy, nausea around food, and major fatigue. All signs of adrenal fatigue and excessive stress.

These symptoms first came about during my relationship and throughout that dating period; taking the lid off what was being stored in my body. On a spiritual level, which I didn't see at the time, my soul was weary, my spiritual connection was dry, and I was trying to move out of my own strength. How did I get there?

You're probably thinking I could have seen the signs earlier, however, it was so subtle to me. I didn't notice until it got to the point where I had to take a step back. It was an awakening to the need for personal boundaries and attentive self-care. L.A. became the place of putting my soul, my life, and my health back together.

Connecting the Dots — *Santa Monica Beach*

Three years later: fast forward to being in L.A. for some time now. I am lying on the beach in Santa Monica, letting the waves be my sound muffler as I let my skin soak in the sun. As I am reflecting, listening, and being present, I hear the word *Hashimoto's* in my mind.

I think, *Hmm, that's interesting.* Another friend of mine—who had been diagnosed as well—comes to mind, and I think, *I will reach out to her.*

As I leave the beach, I decide to call my mom. I stop in my tracks when I hear her say, "I have Hashimoto's. I've had it ever since you were born." I knew my mom dealt with health issues concerning her thyroid, but I never put the dots together. I sat in silence for six months noticing symptoms in my body before that revelation at the beach. My body was communicating, and the connections for my healing were coming. I just had to wait for it.

Two or three months pass by after that day at the beach. Follow me here for a moment as I take you on a quick detour; it will make sense later. I'm reminded of this moment when I was at a conference where I was spoken to about Arizona. From that point forward, I started to see "Arizona" on license plates, on billboards, in dreams, and continued meeting people from Arizona. Random or divinely appointed, I still questioned it myself.

This conference was about six years ago, and the main speaker pointed at me and said, "I see Arizona and a daisy chain link, a network building for you—you are going to lead children out of trauma through dance. First, dance is going to be your avenue of healing through your own trauma."

Arizona was the marker, and it was something I kept in the back of my mind.

Divine Answers — *Lunch With A Friend*

Here I am, grabbing lunch, meeting with a friend I worked for at the beginning of my time in L.A. Her five-year-old son walks in with a T-shirt that says... wait for it... "Arizona." We sit down to begin eating as she shares her story. She starts off by saying, "Cassie, I am from Arizona." I chuckle a little as my eyes open in disbelief. *Of course,* I think.

"A few years back, I was diagnosed with Hashimoto's. Before then, I had overcome an eating disorder." As she continues to share, waves of shock roll through me as her next words hit my core. "I have also survived and experienced sexual assault."

The thread. The narratives. I keep hearing it from different mouths, yet there's a collective experience that has been revealed. Here it is again, the third woman I talked to who told me they had overcome an eating disorder, had issues with their thyroid and had experienced sexual trauma.

As I sat there and listened, I discovered that what I thought was normal living was actually the symptoms of Hashimoto's. I left that conversation with the realization that encountering these women who carry pieces of my story pulled out the truth in me that I could not see yet.

Do you see the dots aligning? That is the beauty of connection; our stories hold pieces of each other and we need community for healing. We need the stories of each other to hold a light up to the places we can't see in ourselves. The connections, the divine encounters—people carry a piece of our healing and I know we all carry a piece of heaven.

Turning Against The Self — *Stories of Women*

I was reading a book on a study done on women who had experienced incest in their upbringing versus those who did not and the overall effect on their immune systems. The study was sparked from the story of a woman who experienced incest in her family and as she got older, she was diagnosed with an auto-immune disorder in one of her retinas. The line, "This was one of many women who had a history of incest and were later diagnosed with an auto-immune disease, a disease that attacks itself—the body," stood out to me. (Van der Kolk, Bessel. *The Body Keeps the Score: Brain, Mind, and Body in the Healing of Trauma*. Penguin Books, 2014.)

What is the body holding that we need help guiding ourselves through?

Part of attuning to our bodies is learning our body's language when it comes in the form of physical symptoms and learning to listen to what it is sharing with us. When we transition into letting our body lead and speak to us, we can embrace parts of ourselves that we may not have known existed. We are invited into a depth that may have been buried for some time.

The more we trust our bodies and can create less resistance in ourselves, the more we can walk in a way that we feel safe and don't have to look for that safety externally. Our body has us, it knows us, and it carries the wisdom and healing that it's waiting to show us.

Parenting the Pain — *Evenings At Home: Healing The Stomach* — *Lazarus Season*

From a young age, I spent some time in bed due to stomach pain. I was excused from exams in school, missed school, and spent days lying in bed from this ongoing occurrence. It was constant, probably chronic, and a memory I do remember from my childhood. Though it looked different, it continued into my adult years. It came in waves. This time, I had to face it all head-on.

"Stomach, your responsibility is to digest food. You don't have to carry anything else," I began to say to myself. "Cassie, I am proud of you. Look at how far you've come," I said to myself while intentionally placing my hand on my stomach.

As I speak, I begin to remember the relationship I've had with my stomach over the years. From childhood, I had consistent digestive issues, lying in bed from what felt like chronic stomach pain. The pain was elevated around stressful situations while staying pretty frequent. When I was at the height of my digestive pain and sensitivity (for a four-month period), like a mother to a little girl, I started my evenings by affirming my body.

I spent time speaking to my body, and speaking to my heart what I wanted to hear from others. But, more importantly, speaking what my body needed to hear from me. My bed would be my security, holding me up as I lay there at night wondering what the next morning would hold. Whatever it held, I chose to still continue to mother those parts of myself that needed nourishment.

I chose to believe, even when most mornings felt heavy, that one day, the depth of this pain would be over. I started taking vigorous notes of what I felt in my body when I woke up, when I ate, and when I went to bed. Choosing to be intentional and attentive to the symptoms, I made a choice to be active in my recovery and gain an understanding of the symptoms I shared with the many other women I read about.

I took my friend from Arizona's advice, and I reached out to her doctor when my symptoms were not lessening. I started with minimal blood tests with my main doctor but took it into my own hands when I was denied further testing because my test results came back "normal." Something else I learned from the women I met.

Their stories carried answers and knowledge for me to piece together my own narrative with my health and body. One woman had to write up her own labs to be specifically tested for different thyroid levels. Other women told me the basic blood test didn't reveal their symptoms, and they spent years working with functional or holistic doctors to find a solution to their underlying issues.

I knew what I was going through was far from normal. However, basic help kept being denied. I had another doctor who never met me, saw my records once, and—in a twenty-minute phone call—immediately suggested antidepressants. Another refused to do further testing because she saw no signs of "issues."

I knew something wasn't right, so I decided to listen to the women I was meeting and to the story of my body to find an answer.

The Results — *Functional Doctor Appointment*

It's finally that day—I've waited six months for this. The test results are in. My symptoms are still periodical nausea, heightened nausea around stressful situations, fatigue, lethargy, and brain fog. When I say fatigue, I mean going to the grocery store was a task that required me to recharge, and sometimes even doing errands almost led to the possibility of passing out.

I'm anxiously waiting in the office at this functional doctor facility recommended by my friend from Arizona. Today was the day when the answers would come, the ones I'd been waiting for. I finally get to hear what is really happening in my body.

"The good news is, you don't have cancer and no autoimmune disorder, such as Hashimoto's, so that is ruled out. There is some inflammation in your body and I do want to do additional testing with your hormones. However, the overarching infection you have is called candida." I pause in relief, yet I am slightly curious about the word "candida." It definitely wasn't as intense as I thought it would be.

From there, she went on to share with me the specialized meal plans, supplements, and information I needed to reset and heal the microbiome in my body.

"If you've been feeling nauseous, exhaustion/fatigue, and brain fog, all those are symptoms common with candida." A piece of clarity hits me. My memory flashes back to all the mornings I faced those symptoms. I begin to see what bio-chemically is happening in my body.

It is about tackling the issue from multiple avenues—the mind, the emotions, the body, and this diagnosis started me on a path of understanding more clearly what was chemically happening in my body.

A few months into the supplements and food protocol, I began to see my appetite returning, the nausea lessening, and slowly, my health returning to my body. Along with the protocol, I researched the causes of candida. I found there were many—one of them being stress. I know my strongest flare-ups or moments of pain came in stressful situations. Dating or interacting with men was quite stressful for me, for example.

Understanding that connection unlocked the mystery, and my journey of clarity continued. Who knows if that caused my body to shut down, but I did know where I was and where I could go. Behind physical symptoms lies the emotional turmoil.

Hormones — *Doctor Consultation*

"Sexual abuse speeds up their [abused, isolated girls with incest histories] biological clocks and the secretion of sex hormones. Early in puberty, the abused girls had three to five times the levels of testosterone and androstenedione—the hormones that fuel sexual desire—as did the girls in the control group. Researchers recruited eighty-four girls referred by the District of Columbia Department of Social Services who had a confirmed history of sexual abuse by a family member. They were matched with a comparison group of eighty-two girls of the same age, race, socio-economic status, and family constellation who had not been abused. The sexually abused showed abnormalities in their stress hormone responses, had an earlier onset of puberty, and accumulated a host of different, seemingly unrelated psychiatric diagnoses." (Van der Kolk, Bessel. *The Body Keeps the*

Score: Brain, Mind, and Body in the Healing of Trauma. Penguin Books, 2014.)

"As you can see on your lab results, you have extremely high levels of testosterone. That can be a result of stress, eating habits, or abnormalities in the body. We can see from your cortisol output that you are far above the range of normalcy," my functional doctor began to share. I am listening intently as the doctor continues. "Usually, most people experience high cortisol levels in the morning, and it goes down throughout the day. However, your cortisol levels stay the same all through the day, meaning your body is in constant fight or flight mode." As I studied traumatic experiences, I learned that a new default system is set in place, and life is filtered through that new setting.

"The brain doesn't know the difference between psychological and emotional stress, and it looks like you are experiencing both," my doctor goes on. I sit there, seeing the stories I read, the people I've met, and the emotional and physical ties to my story merging together in my head. It is all beginning to make sense, and my discipline now is helping my body breathe, relax, and no longer live in a place of chronic stress.

Continued Restoration — *Faith In The Marketplace Conference*

"God, I ask that you heal the trauma that still resides in Cassie's body. Would you wash out the remaining effects of her childhood that have affected her body physically?" I open my eyes, wondering how this woman knows this. She is calm yet stern as my gaze scans her face, looking for a sense of understanding. What she is saying is exactly what I am walking through.

My hands hold onto hers, eyes attentive, as she speaks words of refreshment and refinement to my soul. I am attending a seminar on faith and industry work as a friend nudges me to receive prayer. "I know you asked to pray for direction. However, this is what I felt like the Lord wants to address." I knew she was in tune with what the Creator was doing and what the Creator knew I needed.

Even as we begin to address the physical symptoms, when we address the root, the emotional turmoil, the symptoms slowly evaporate and have no life source. The more we heal internally, we will recognize a shift in our body. It's in addressing those stored-up emotions and internal barriers, we see liberation from ongoing physical pain.

Reflection

- How would you describe your relationship with your body? Are you aware of any ongoing physical pain?

- Have you noticed any emotions trying to surface in your body recently? Ways your body is trying to communicate with you?

- As you hear part of my journey—the medical side—does anyone come to mind? Write those names down.

- In the next two weeks, reach out to those people—you never know what they carry that can release part of your own healing.

Next Steps

Take a few moments to read, process, and journal the following questions. Let the questions help guide you in reaching out to the right people and in finding more clarity in where you are at in your relationship with your body.

Tools

- Speaking to your body

  - "I am listening."

  - "I got you."

  - "I am here."

  - "What do you need?"

  - "I am proud of you. I see you. You are safe. You are beautiful."

- Journal

- Writing down similar reactions you see coming up in your body; physical symptoms—"tracking/triggers/logging your body reactions."

- Praying/blessing your body

  - Colossians 2:9; John 14:27

  - Podcast

    - Mel Robbins & Neuroscientist Tara – Manifestation, Visualization and Affirmations

    - https://www.youtube.com/watch?v=Uzt-Woc3CVk

Book/Podcast Recommendations
- "The Body Keeps the Score" – Bessel Van Der Kolk

- "This is why you feel lost & unhappy in life" – Gabor Mate – Mindset Theory Podcast

Notes
- We need the stories of each other to hold a light up to the places we can't see in ourselves.

- In the study conducted of women who experienced incest growing up versus a group who had not, there was a woman who developed an autoimmune disease in one of her eyes. "This was one of many women who had a history of incest and were later diagnosed with an autoimmune disease, a disease that attacks itself—the body." (The Body Keeps The Score)

- The more we trust our bodies and create less resistance in ourselves, the more we can walk in a way that we feel safe and don't have to look for that safety externally.

- Behind those physical symptoms lies the emotional turmoil. It's in addressing the emotions stored up and/or blocked in our lives in hopes of seeing liberation from ongoing physical pain.

Awakening: Seeing clearly to liberate

"Awakening is not changing who you are but discarding who you are not." –
Deepak Chopra

The provision we look for doesn't always come as we expect. Provision can look like people, it can look like books, it can even look like hearing that line on a TV show, or overhearing someone say something in a coffee shop that speaks to your situation. Provision comes in varieties and it is food for our soul and our key back to wholeness.

I started reading *It Didn't Start With You*, a book that gave me keys to unlock a level of understanding of my family history. "What isn't spoken about in the family will get passed down to the next generations." There were stories upon stories of individuals who started experiencing physical, mental, and/or emotional symptoms either from a young age or at a designated age.

The enlightening stories were those who experienced symptoms at a certain age, to later find out, in their family history, that someone had passed away or experienced those same exact symptoms at that exact age. In a sense, it was like subconsciously passing a baton to the next generation.

"Unresolved traumas from our family history spill into successive generations, blending into our emotions, reactions, and choices in ways we never think to question. We assume these experiences originate with us. With their true source out of sight, we're often unable to differentiate what is ours from what is not." (Wolynn, Mark. *It Didn't Start with You: How Inherited Family Trauma Shapes Who We Are and How to End the Cycle*. Penguin Books, 2017, pp. 58.)

Bert Hellinger, a psychotherapist, explains that we share a family consciousness with biological family members. We relive or practically "inherit" the past, in which case traumatic events leave a mark on the entire family system, and family members unconsciously repeat the "sufferings of the past." (Wolynn, Mark. *It Didn't Start with You: How Inherited Family Trauma Shapes Who We Are and How to End the Cycle*. Penguin Books, 2017, pp. 44.)

I knew my fear went deep. It felt like a stronghold over my life, something that I didn't obtain simply from my own experiences. The mystery for me was, where did it derive? It carried a weight that had taken me years of unraveling and years to climb out of. Piece by piece, I was putting the segments together of my family history, family circumstances, and my own story. I knew it was more than me, and this book became my provision to get to the core.

No Longer Hiding — *Conversation With A Close Family Member*

"No one knows besides you," a family member confides in me. I listen, letting what they share sink in. "I was molested and never told anyone. No one in the family knows." In slight shock and disbelief, I watch the words cross my mind again.

How does no one know? I think. *Maybe they only shared because I asked, but that isn't good to carry.*

This family member is a pivotal person in my life—one who I've been around my whole upbringing; a parental figure.

Is my body experiencing their story that was never told? Or are there still more pieces of my own? I question.

Pondering the untold stories from one family member to the next, I began to see the stronghold my body held around men had many contributors. This generational story was one of the keys. Those unspoken traumas were now in my language, my emotions, and my body.

Getting to the Core — *Timing*

The mystery with healing is it doesn't seem to happen in a particular order. It has its own timing. When you try to look for an answer in one area, you seem to get an answer in another. We can dig and dig, yet healing comes at the timing it wants to. When the time is right, the core foundation, the depth of our being that has been buried for years, will begin to bubble up.

When we know the core foundation, we can start to see where all the symptoms of that core pain connect. We start to see pieces come together as to why we react the way we do and, most importantly, why we view the world the way we do.

Unveiling — *Counseling Session*

"It's another day, and I am at the grocery store. I face a similar tension as I see a man down the aisle. Do I go down the aisle? I don't want to. I begin to debate with myself. The same story goes for a male cashier; I don't want to go down that aisle. This is the usual dialogue in my head in daily situations. What is that?" I asked my counselor.

"Cassie, this is all connected. From what you saw with your mother growing up, the absence of your father, the generational trauma passed down—it all ties into your present actions toward men. Another piece of this fear is finally unlocked," my counselor said. Her comment connected my past to the present body reactions I was experiencing.

"I started to have this consistent dream that feels similar to memories of my childhood," I explain. "One dream in particular reminds me of a real-life situation at a daycare I once attended. In elementary school, I had two experiences as a young girl at that daycare that I think added to my fear of not feeling capable of speaking up around men. I never saw the correlation until speaking to you about it now," I said.

I had a dream that a man wanted me to have sex with him. Similar dreams started to come up more often as memories resurfaced. Slowly, small pieces were putting themselves together.

The fear I carried around men was becoming more tangible for me to see as I recognized my history and continued to walk through constant triggers. As I spent many years focusing on external things happening to me as my body was constantly reactive, the invitation to switch from external to internal presented itself.

Now the focus was facing the internal disconnect that started to form within me. I was now invited to turn my gaze to the internal separation birthed by trauma.

Digging In — *My Morning Routine: Lazarus Season Continued*

It's morning, and I am lying in bed, already facing a whirlwind of thoughts as I try to imagine what I am going to eat for breakfast. I say out loud, "God, I surrender my meal times to you. You can tell me when you want me to eat."

Immediately, I hear, "Talk to Bree." My brows raise, and my eyes tighten as I think, *Did you hear my question? What do I eat?* Feeling slightly irritated and confused, I decided to reach out to Bree.

Bree was a friend of mine with whom I did non-profit work after college. We had an instant bond. Bree is a marriage and family therapist who has been trained in EMDR (Eye Movement Desensitization and Reprocessing Therapy). Little did I know at the time Bree would guide me in facing my cracked internal foundation.

Later that day, I gave her a call.

"Cassie, as you share with me what is going on, first, it has nothing to do with food. It's something emotional your body is releasing," Bree said. That wasn't the first time I heard that. "Also, it sounds like the root you're now addressing is internal." I am pacing back and forth in the parking lot, waiting to hear what comes next.

"From what I'm hearing, it sounds like you don't trust yourself." As simple as it sounds, my body is already starting to respond. My knees clench, and my stomach twists as a wave of nausea hits me. "Cassie, there it is," she says to me as she hears the echoes of my pain.

Those words showed me the center of the collage of my pain. The way I coped growing up and how I functioned in the world was through creating a distinct separation from myself. I knew this was the internal invitation to build that connection and trust once again.

The awakening is recognizing that we hold the power we need to heal. In the journey of coming back to ourselves, our bodies, and our voices, we build a relationship with our bodies that will forever be our security. The core reality is there is external fear. However, internal fear is where it stems from. Once we feel secure in how we manage ourselves and approach our bodies, we can walk into situations with a sense of confidence, knowing we are deeply connected to ourselves.

I had the impression that my healing was in confronting men when, simultaneously, the invitation was for me to do the internal work through the barriers that kept me disconnected from myself. That disconnect can give birth to self-hate, self-rejection, and more. When we address the core, we come out of the cocoon of our shadow and into the light of our intended being.

Reflection

- How would you define trust, and what does that look like with your own connection to yourself and your body?

- What may hinder you from building trust with yourself?

- In what ways have you grown in trusting yourself more? What tools have helped you get there? How do you want to see that continue?

Next Steps

- Read *It Didn't Start With You* by Mark Woylnn

  - Exercises to guide you through understanding and mapping out generational trauma and family history

Notes

- The mystery with healing is, when you think you have found the root, it sometimes will lead you to the foundation of that root system.

- With trauma and life experiences, we not only become disconnected from ourselves, but we also lose a sense of safety in our own bodies.

- Your body will guide you to the root. Your body will also guide you to your healing.

- As we grow in trusting ourselves, we grow in confidence and approach life in a way where we know who we are and that we are capable.

Resources

- Psychology Today

  - Great resource for potential counselors and therapists.

    - https://www.psychologytoday.com/us

- Sozo Ministry (Faith-Based)

  - Inner-healing ministry that brings out the root and barriers keeping us from being connected to the Creator and ourselves. This ministry is available at different churches as well. However, this is the home base of where it started: http://bethelsozo.com

Part 2: The Internal Mending

Re-introducing: Connecting back to yourself

"The most terrifying thing is to accept oneself completely." – C.G. Jung

When we walk through the pain, our bodies are detoxing, and we face internal barriers to returning back to ourselves. We are invited to look at ourselves with a new narrative and get rid of the old, and it may feel like we are introducing a stranger to us. We might have lived a long time believing certain things about ourselves and treating ourselves a certain way, acting out of self-protection.

I had much to learn about who I actually was. Outside of survival, outside of the pain, who are we? It is a complex idea to realize that the trauma we experience externally, our bodies hold internally. As we start the journey of reconnecting and uncovering the real us, it starts here—working with the big words (we know them already): self-hatred and self-acceptance.

Introducing Self Hatred — *Elementary School Recess*

I can still see the scene clearly in my mind as if it were yesterday. I am slowly walking toward the blacktop, making my way to my group of friends as other kids run around for recess when a thought crosses my mind. *I wish I was like that girl.*

It was like an invasive thought, dominating the others. My body starts to slump, my face starts to melt, and my heart starts to wish it was in another body.

Similar memories started to pile atop each other after that moment. I remember that thought became more consistent as I slowly wanted to be like other girls rather than wanting to be myself. This narrative continued as I got older, deepening a wedge within me. The birth of what became a taste of self-hatred.

I didn't like myself, yet I couldn't remember when that decision was made. As I look back, it wasn't a conscious decision that I made to no longer like myself. It was a choice, a mechanism I started to choose. As a young girl in the house I lived in, I witnessed abuse, cultural differences, abandonment, and more. Instead of being able to acknowledge what was happening, I suppressed it and took that anger out on myself.

I didn't understand a lot of the turmoil that happened within my home, so I processed it as "I am the problem." I would get frustrated with myself, as a root of not feeling good enough, because I didn't know how to engage with what was going on. What young kid knows how to do that at such a young age? Blaming myself, attaching what was happening to my worth, and therefore, creating an agreement with self-hatred to solidify its residency in my life.

I didn't realize I was separating internally. I just knew I wanted to be like other girls, someone who wasn't me, and that was a sign that there was more turmoil in my childhood environment. As I got older, self-hatred showed up differently in my life. It was still there, but that didn't mean it would stay forever.

Hand in hand with self-hatred came dissociation. A sense of walking away from myself out of protection and an instinctual response. "Dissociation is a common symptom in traumatic stress reactions. The overwhelming force of traumatic events overpowers our existing coping mechanisms. (Van der Kolk, 2014.) For those unable to physically escape, dissociation provides a psychological exit from the horror of the traumatic event." (Heshmat, Shahram. What is the Dissociative Mind? *Psychology Today*, 10 February 2021, https://psychologytoday.com/usblog/science -choice/202102/what-is-the-dissociative-mind.)

As I slowly stepped away from myself, I found an escape as a way to disappear from the environment around me. I turned to an external focus, choosing the thoughts of others to decide who I was and who I wasn't. I lost my voice, coping with what felt hard to face in my upbringing. In return, I looked to others to fill my sense of identity and worth.

How do we move out of that? Out of self-hatred? For me, I first acknowledged that there was self-hatred and dissociation present in my life. Second, I embarked on a committed discipline to learn tools and techniques for cultivating self-acceptance from within versus external validation. In order to take steps toward self-acceptance, ultimately, self-hatred must be dismantled. We are invited to break the layers of its foundation to come back home to who we really are.

Acknowledging The Critic — *Prayer Ministry Training*

You are a fucking idiot. I can't believe you are late again. Everyone is going to look at you and treat you a certain way. Look at what you did.

A tear starts to roll down the side of my face as these thoughts carry on in my head. I am driving to a prayer ministry training, and I am running late. Yes, you heard it right, a prayer ministry training; and simultaneously, I am in need of help and prayer. I am looking for parking while trying to pull myself together, but I know I am already in a mood. This internal dialogue is a little insight into my intense inner critic.

That day when I heard those thoughts run through my mind, I thought it was normal as similar scenarios continued to happen. Normal? Absolutely not. This was the residue of self-hatred popping up in the later years of my life, yet it was now requiring my effort to dismantle.

Self-hatred is a real thing. "Encompassing continuous feelings of guilt, inadequacy, and low self-esteem," as Psychology Today defines it. "Beyond triggers, the root can be traced to environmental circumstances, such as hypercritical parenting or personality traits like perfectionism." (Psychology Today. https://www.psychologytoday.com/us/basics/self-hatred.)

First, it is key to acknowledge where self-hatred shows up in our lives. Do we see it in our inner dialogue about who we are, or does it come up in self-sabotage, not thinking we have value? Around what settings or people have we noticed its presence and its voice?

For instance, I experienced it both ways—internally and externally. Internally, as shown in the story above, I always had an intense inner critic, one that felt more abusive than helpful. It was like a constant judge in my head, and in group settings, it was as if my life was being narrated while I was trying to break free of its story.

Externally, it started with me wanting to be like other girls and not wanting to be me. I could somehow see the beauty in others while being blind to what I carried. That was an indicator that I didn't know or see me. After we acknowledge where self-hatred shows up in our lives, we can begin to tear away its roots.

The shift comes in choosing another perspective; even in subtle ways. As I got older, I continued to compare myself to other women. The transition in my perspective came in seeing this comparison as an invitation to see myself. If I saw myself comparing, it was less about the other woman. Instead, I asked, what does she carry that I would like to see in myself?

Also, what we observe in another is within us. A lot of times, comparison is showing us what is already within—we just need help tapping into it. As Mel Robbins would say, "Jealousy is just blocked creativity." Here was tool number one, beginning to forgive "me" for the ways I saw myself through those small shifts in perspective.

Tool number two: building self-acceptance with intention and a committed choice. Invest in getting to know yourself again. What do you like to do? When was the last time you took yourself on a date? Through this process you are no longer living your life trying to be everyone else, to feel a sense of belonging or love, but instead are finding that love for yourself again. That belonging, that acceptance you will find, is already within you, already given by the Creator.

Tool number three: connecting to a higher power. However you choose to connect spiritually, through meditation or prayer, that time with the One who created you will also reflect back to you who you are with a clear lens that is no longer tainted from trauma, fear, and uncertainty. Having that spiritual connection is a great foundation. Learning techniques and reading books to help reconnect you to your sense of self and your self-worth, coupled with the spiritual piece, will ultimately bring you to self-acceptance.

Now, when we start to see self-hatred try to voice itself, we can decide how we are going to engage with it. How will we change the thought, and how will we begin to pour our energy into a fresh, new perspective? Once something has come to the light, it holds less power, and self-hatred, the layers, will loosen their grip.

The End of Hate's Beginning — *Sozo Inner-Healing Session*

"Cassie, is there a person named self-hatred living inside of you? When did self-hatred come in?"

What the hell is this? I start thinking.

I'm tentatively sitting in a chair as I let the woman across from me lead me through an inner-healing session. The next moment, without even recognizing it, I start speaking and say, "At the age of zero."

How do I know that? I murmur to myself.

"We are going to invite self-hatred to leave and no longer stay with you," this woman says.

"This feels the hardest to let go of," I say. "It feels like it is a part of me."

In that therapy session, I learned not only can self-hatred be generationally passed down, but it can also be a spirit that attaches to us, even in the womb. Generationally and spiritually we can invite a spirit of self-hatred into our lives by agreeing with lies. It can also be passed down from one generation to another.

How could I invite "self-hatred" into my life at the age of zero? It is the circumstances, the environment, and even the mental state of our parents that contribute to what we experience in the womb. All that to say, as I got older, I wondered why this feeling of hate felt so hard to break.

You may not remember, but my mom and dad broke two rules in their relationship. One being my mom wasn't Greek and the second one being they weren't married. It wasn't until I was older that I found out my mom was denied entry into the house when visiting my dad while she was pregnant with me. The cultural differences and opinions were felt even in the womb. The rejection my mother felt was also passed down to me.

We carry the emotions, and those impressions, with us, wondering why and when we turned against ourselves. A lot of times those negative emotions came in contact with us when we were young. The invitation now is to be aware and actively choose to pour into a new way of thinking, a new story of who we really are.

Filling Up The Cup of Worth — *Nothing Hidden Ministries*

"Cassie, I want you to hold up this mirror and start naming what you love about yourself." I anxiously grab a mirror and begin speaking as I am sitting in front of a group of people. Each of us is attending a different exercise tailored to us. I start to speak the opposite of what I would usually let run freely in my head.

I begin the process of building a new thought pathway toward myself. "Cassie, I really love how you value others, and you yourself are valuable." I awkwardly laugh and smile. I keep speaking, thinking everyone is probably like, "Wow, this is so basic," yet when I look around at my group, everyone's eyes are attentively watching, and their posture is intentionally leaned in.

From that moment, I took that exercise with me. On days I noticed the old narrative trying to chime in, I started talking instead. I made it a discipline to pour into a "new cup" with comments I liked about me; to build a stronger narrative, one that would silence the other.

The Fruit of Discipline — *Morning Routine*

Cassie, you look beautiful. I pause as I hear that thought again.

You look really beautiful; I mean, look at you. I pause.

Is that really me saying that? I question my own thoughts while gazing into the mirror.

Woah, that was a different thought, I commented back to myself in my head.

I noticed some days like this, hearing what felt abnormal was slowly becoming my new internal dialogue toward myself. Showing me the progress of the work that I committed to at Nothing Hidden Ministries. The commitment to loving, seeing, and acknowledging me in the journey of self-acceptance.

It is a journey, and as you invest in yourself, you will see those sweet surprises, too. Really, the process will show you how strong you really are and how much stronger you are for walking through the life that was trying to taint you. While self-hatred tries to create separation, self-acceptance, in conjunction with self-care, is our guide on the road back to ourselves. Self-acceptance can look different to us all. However, it is the choice and the discipline to invest, commit, and value who we are. It looks like getting to know ourselves and what makes us, *us*.

It also looks like forgiveness for decisions, for ways we have spoken negatively about ourselves, and for ways we have passed up our own needs out of neglect. It's like telling a friend (ourselves) what we love about them and committing to doing that to rebuild a connection that has been lost.

I have attached workbooks below that facilitate activities, ideas, and prompts to help you get to know yourself all over again. Re-connecting to yourself is a process and I am still in the business of facing more to work through.

My sweet roommate in my late twenties once told me, "God weeps over the idea that you do not like what God created." Burned in my memory now, this comment reminds me that God created me the way I am, and I am the one getting in the way of my own healing, growth, and life because I reject the Creator's work.

What God creates, God does with intention. May that remind you how much your story is needed. There is one you, only you, and I believe others are waiting in need of your story.

Reflection

- Have you seen any form of self-hatred show up in your own life? What has helped you in tearing down its foundation?

- What do you think about self-acceptance? Where are you in the process of accepting your full self?

- Have you experienced self-rejection? Have words, memories, or events hindered how you look at your body?

Next Steps

- Take some time to journal and think through the questions written above. I encourage you to also look into the articles listed below for further knowledge on self-hatred and self-acceptance.

Resources

- Tools in understanding Self-hatred & Self-loathing and overcoming its power

  - https://www.psychologytoday.com/us/basics/self-hatred#what-causes-self-hatred

- A Guide to Cultivating Self Love – Ph.D. Jade WU

  - https://www.psychologytoday.com/us/basics/self-hatred#what-causes-self-hatred

- Self-Love; Workbook for Women by Megan Logan

Notes

- The trauma we see externally, our body holds internally.

- Self-hatred is defined as "continuous feelings of guilt, inadequacy, and low self-esteem." Its roots can come from environmental factors and personality traits and can be passed down spiritually or generationally.

- In dismantling self-hatred and coming to self-acceptance, we need to break the layers of its foundation to come back home to who we really are.

- Self-acceptance is the invitation to take the road back to ourselves. It is the choice and the discipline to invest, commit, and value who we are. It looks like getting to know yourself and what makes you, *you*.

- "God weeps over the idea that you do not like what He created." There is one you, only you, and what God creates, God does with intention.

Returning: Finding safety in self & breaking free from self-rejection

"Because true belonging only happens when we present our authentic, imperfect selves to the world, our sense of belonging can never be greater than our level of self-acceptance." – Brene Brown

Returning to our bodies sounds like a paradox. We are our body, yet we can be living in separation from ourselves. We talked about self-hatred, dissociation, and how that creates distance within our relationship with our body, and yet another layer of that separation is self-rejection.

Self-rejection can be built off of many factors; the opinion of others, the opinion of ourselves, words we heard growing up in and out of the home, and even the societal manipulation of what we are "supposed" to look like. In returning to ourselves, we first must connect to our bodies in a healthy way, and that requires us to see ourselves in a healthy way. The way we see our bodies affects how we build a relationship with ourselves as well as how well we can connect with others. A way of creating deeper intimacy and companionship with our bodies is through first seeing ourselves through a lens of grace and affirmation.

The Old Narrative — *Day At Home*

I am trying to figure out what to wear before getting ready to leave the house. It is one of those days. I'm feeling indecisive. My feet slowly carry me out of my room as I approach my roommate sitting on the couch. "Do I look too thin; do I look gross?" I ask.

My question is desperate for some form of validation as my body is hungry to feel free from the tormenting internal dialogue to be itself. "Cassie, ever since I met you, I never thought you looked unhealthy, I just knew your frame was more petite," my roommate responds.

"You look anorexic."

"You are so thin."

"What happened to you?"

These were some of the comments I received throughout the years. I didn't think twice about my weight until people started pointing it out to me. Without fully being aware, I eventually let those comments sink in and form the way I looked at my body. I started to hide. I found clothes that covered how small my legs were and T-shirts that would cover a lot of skin.

My narrative of being "too thin" formed, and I started to compare my body type to those around me. In time, I started to see myself as sick, unhealthy, and not good. I noticed as I partnered with the thoughts of others and the ones that developed in my head I was choosing to reject my body. I had another invitation to break down the layers that had contributed to an altered image of myself.

One of the layers was comparison. Comparison is a form of self-rejection. We compare when we think we lack. We lack when we don't know who we are or what we possess. I've always considered myself freakishly thin, and I've always thought other women had beautiful bodies. I constantly wondered what it was like to be in someone else's body because my own felt like a stranger.

The reality was that my body carried the deepest gift—the container to hold my own soul and spirit. My body knew me best. Little did I know that when I began to choose my body and come back to settle into myself, I would see there was no need to compare. When we see that we have abundance within ourselves, there is no lack, and there's no need to reach outward.

Now, what does it look like to start a journey of reconnecting to ourselves and reconciling ourselves?

Breaking Shame — *Nothing Hidden Ministries Conference*

"I have an exercise for everyone," the speaker informs us. Eighty of us sitting in small groups wait attentively as we endure day two of eight-hour training. My body, slightly tense, is balancing the comfort and discomfort I begin to feel from these exposing sessions. We are going into topics of trauma, sexuality, and inner healing, with the goal of deeper freedom.

"Tonight, when you go home, I want you to stand in front of your bathroom mirror naked and speak life to the places of your body that you have rejected." I look around the room, my mind a little perplexed. An interesting assignment, but I'm deciding to trust it has a purpose. "In the feedback we receive from the couples who go through this conference, a main issue that arises in marriages is women feeling shame over their bodies during sex. Our hope is through the resources we share with you this weekend, including this exercise, that the shame will break off you."

Our relationship with our bodies is even evident to those around us. Our bodies will show us (if we make space for it and let it) where we need reconciliation. It's in trusting our body to lead us in our healing and the courage to walk it out.

The healing is in becoming a friend to our body again. The sooner we actively choose connection with ourselves, the sooner we have the chance to live fully in our power. Our bodies have carried us through and experienced everything we've experienced. It's like having a best friend from the moment we were born.

Tapping In — *Dance Session Exchange*

"Breathe in for four counts and out for four counts." My chest struggles to open up as I breathe in for four, listening to the guidance of our friend in her living room. "This technique helps our breath guide us versus our minds as we move."

My chest resists the pressure it feels as it tries to dig deeper for air. *I look absolutely ridiculous. Is this really effective?* Before it was my turn to go, I didn't realize what this moment was about to teach me. "OK, your turn Cassie."

My feet hesitantly walk to the center of the room to engage in breathing and movement. Slowly I begin to take up space as my arms and legs expand in different directions. I surrender my "performance" mindset and "what I should look like." As I do, I notice something. A tear crawls down my face as I continue to move; then little pools of water gather around my eyes the longer I dance.

Shortly after, I walk from the center of the room and take a moment to myself. I know I am hitting something. Grief. My body grieving how I see my own self, how I live in it yet neglect it, and the desire of wanting the war in myself to be over.

Self-rejection keeps us in a place of resistance. The sooner we peel back the barriers, the thoughts, and the behaviors, the sooner we can continue on the journey of settling back into who we are and move from a place of certainty and groundedness.

The Internal Cry — *Dinner With Friends*

It's my first year in Los Angeles, and I am sitting at a restaurant getting ready to leave with my group of friends when an email notification alerts my phone. "Photos just in." Mind you, this is my first photoshoot/head-shot session ever. I hit the notification, opened up the document, and showed a friend. What starts as excitement ends with me abruptly putting my phone away.

"SK, can I talk to you?" I ask as I pull my friend aside. She looks at me, and immediately my body bends over. I don't know how or why, but the tears rapidly come. It all feels beyond exposing and embarrassing, yet the thoughts swarm, and all I feel is the gut-wrenching feeling of inadequacy.

I knew this moment was an invitation to have a little pep talk with myself. Time to combat the initial reaction to seeing my own photo. My dialogue went a little like this: "Sweet Cassie, first, you are so beautiful. You carry beauty in the way you are, not in what you put on. Second, I see you and accept you. Keep living *koukla*, as my θεία would say, if you can only see what you carry, you would know there is no limit. I am proud of you."

In being in tune with our inner self-dialogue and our body's emotions, our body no longer has to carry the weight of the past. Moments like the story I shared above may happen again, but the growth point is being able to be present in that moment and then follow up with yourself.

"What does Cassie need?" and "I see you, Cassie." A big part of the journey is building up a new dialogue, so our bodies no longer have to function from a place it learned in survival, in trauma and in childhood.

There are many tools, books, and workshops to help address self-rejection. Some I will share here. I've continued to implement how I speak over my body, how I address self-rejecting thoughts, and how movement-based classes keep me moving forward. I highly encourage guided movement that focuses on embracing your body, to guide you in showing compassion towards yourself and in helping you build a sense of safety within your body again.

Reflection

- Where have you noticed self-rejection coming up for you?

- Can you identify self-rejecting thoughts and behaviors in how you see and treat your body?

- What has been helpful for you thus far in moving through self-rejection?

Next Steps

- Take some time to reflect and respond to the questions listed above. Write out any memories or moments that come to mind as you read through some of my own personal stories.

- Look into one of the options in the resources listed below—taking a movement class or downloading a guide of exercises in reconciling back to your body.

Resources

- Nothing Hidden Ministries

  - https://ecourses.nothinghidden.com/courses/single-life-work shop-crash-course

    - This is a free crash course from the ministry I spoke of in this chapter, where I found the tools for loving my body and building a healthy connection with myself and others.

- Webinars—American Dance Movement Therapy

  - https://www.adta.org/webinars

- Self-Reclaimed Workshops & Education

  - https://www.instagram.com/selfreclaimed/

Notes
- The way we see our bodies steers how we build a relationship with ourselves.

- We compare when we think we lack. When we see that we have abundance within ourselves, there is no lack, and there's no need to reach outward for intended internal security.

- The healing is in becoming a friend to our body again. The sooner we actively choose connection with ourselves over warring with ourselves, that is when we begin to start living fully in our power.

Attunement: Listening to my inner child and befriending my body

"And I said to my body softly, 'I want to be your friend.' It took a long breath and replied, 'I've been waiting my whole life for this.'" – Nayyirah Waheed

A long the path of building a relationship with our bodies, we will face the younger parts of ourselves that need reassurance. Within each of us lives a younger version of ourselves, our inner child, which lives from a default setting; viewing the world and self from the environment it has evolved in.

There are pieces of ourselves that need reassurance and nourishment due to what we lacked growing up. These overwhelming life experiences can keep us frozen in underdeveloped emotional states. Our inner child is still part of us; holding onto scars of the past. Those areas show up in our present life when not attended to, and if we are not aware it can cause havoc.

Tear Down The Walls — *Prayer Ministry Session*

"Cassie, is a person named "Numb" living inside you? If you feel something in your body, let me know." As I notice the therapist combine spiritual and psychological approaches to healing, I listen to the question again. Seconds later, I notice the hair on my arms rise.

"I feel very cold," I say. The temperature drastically shifts around me.

"Cassie, how long has Numb been living with you?"

"Since the age of two," my lips speak as if they know before me.

The therapist explains to me that when we see or experience a traumatic event at a young age and are unable to process an emotion, it becomes a parent to us to keep us safe.

"Cassie, I am going to invite Jesus to come and take Numb home with Him."

OK, not sure how that's going to work.

"Numb, you don't have to be Cassie's parent anymore. Jesus can fill that space," she says.

Next thing I know, I am hunched over. The well is breaking. My eyes give birth to floods of tears. My arms try to grasp something that feels stable. Walking through this pain is the only way of letting it come out of my body, and I know it's that time to pour out.

Sometimes even before we can acknowledge the inner child within us, there are emotions we must address that have carried us through seasons of our lives. Those emotions, such as numbing out and suppressing, can preface the path of reconnecting to our bodies, to the child within us, and more entirely to ourselves.

When we acknowledge that "numbness" and "suppression" were our ways of coping as a child—but we now have another way to process as an adult—we can begin to experience our emotions and process them with our bodies instead of shutting down. The more we speak, the less our body has to carry. A big part of the journey is building up that inner child so our bodies no longer have to function from a place of survival and trauma in childhood.

In my own journey of connecting with my inner child, each layer of my healing invited me to show up differently and more presently. I was beginning to see through work, through friendships and relationships that I was functioning from little Cassie; helpless, anxious, and unsure what would be stable.

I was living in two versions of myself, one from the wounded place and the other from the more healed version; the adult Cassie.

Meeting Me — *Counseling Session*

"Cassie, I want you to imagine you are talking to your younger self. How old is she?" my therapist asks. I take in rhythmic breaths as I lay back in the chair, and my eyelids become the backdrop of this mind-led movie. There I am, visualizing my younger self, and I see a 12-year-old girl staring at the ocean. Her hair is combed by the wind, body is grounded like a statue as she stares into the horizon, waiting for something. She isn't upset or mad—she looks a little lifeless.

"What do you want to say to her?" my therapist asks me. I am fascinated by her because she seems determined yet lost. She seems to not know who she is.

"This little girl doesn't know her power." I feel a coat of sadness cover me when looking at her, and I say what first comes to mind. "Cassie, you are special. You are you. A valuable, brave individual. It's not your fault for what happened in our family. You are not forgotten. I am paying attention to you; I do see you."

A warmth crawled from her face to her body. Life starts to bring breath back into her chest, and I can see her lips turn into a smile, which looks like the first one she has had in a while. I sit there in silence with little Cassie, letting her say what she wants. I can tell she needs comfort and assurance that she is going to be okay.

"Cassie, we are going to leave the beach. Say goodbye to the younger version of yourself." I do not want to go at first. I don't want to leave her, I want to help her. This is where the journey of recognizing there is a little girl still in me started. A little girl who is looking for security. I had to comfort that part of myself into restoration.

I wouldn't have thought that events in my childhood would later affect how I function in the day-to-day world. It makes sense when you read about it, but to live it, I just thought the past was in the past. I didn't really think the past would still be in me. I was able to experience the process of walking out of the effects of my past and attuning to the child within me to address those needs.

I've heard people preach on Sundays, "Let the past go. Let the old self go like the Israelites did in the wilderness." I kept leaving those sermons defeated because I thought, *What am I doing wrong if I believe I've let my past go, but it still feels like it's within me?* As I started my journey outside of those sermons, I realized we were telling people to do something but not showing them how. It was through the narratives of others, professional help, and lots of reading that I learned the "how" and the importance of our inner child work.

What does that look like? To attune to the inner child within us? It's in learning how to parent the inner child within ourselves and bringing that part of us back to life while emotionally maturing those wounded places. This example and format my therapist gave me was a template for future interactions I would have in attuning to my inner child.

Acknowledging Little Cassie — *Counseling Conversation*

"Why do I keep overthinking this?" I ask my counselor. I am in my head about what to say, how to respond, and what to do with this guy I am attracted to. Normal, right? I'm thinking through what to do next. But to me, it feels a little weightier. This isn't even a huge life decision. I've had harder conversations with what felt like bigger decisions. Yet, I began to feel paralyzed by my own analysis. Overthinking and too much introspection.

"Why does it seem hard to decide what to do next?" I pose another question.

"Cassie, that constant overthinking and constant worry of being in your head is little Cassie. Little Cassie didn't get the environment to grow into her autonomy and decision-making skills. We need the Holy Spirit to come into the situation for little Cassie to break this pattern of anxious overthinking," my counselor informs me. "It's through opportunities like these that we become aware of little Cassie, acknowledge the pattern, and begin to mature and heal this area."

It was like a veil was torn before my eyes. I didn't have the awareness before to see that I was living in an old place, the wounded place when facing directional choices for my future. Mind you, this is just a man, but still, it felt scary to me. Another highlight in my healing journey. The little girl in me is still looking for reassurance; it comes in different forms, but the more I choose to attend to her, the more I will solidify a deep connection within myself and, therefore, can take autonomy of my life.

The awareness we build in being attuned to ask the inner child in us what it needs gives us the ultimate liberation in knowing we don't have to live from a wounded place. We can live in the present. "If the reaction is bigger than the current situation, we are responding from the past," my counselor would remind me.

Being aware and acknowledging these feelings as we walk ourselves through, will bring us into greater clarity with ourselves and our bodies.

Reflection

- When you hear my stories of my inner child work, do any memories or thoughts come to mind?

- In what situations do you see your inner child coming up and trying to grab your attention?

- What tools have helped you thus far in your journey of healing the younger parts of yourself?

Next Steps

- Take some time to journal with the reflection questions provided above. I also encourage further reading to learn more about inner child work and how it affects our present-day life. I've provided a book reference below.

- Another great tool for building awareness is taking note when a situation arises and your response seems bigger than the situation. These were the questions I began to ask myself: "Little Cassie, what are you feeling? What do you need?" I would listen, be aware, and reassure the little child within me. The process here is the more we actively attend to the inner child, the less intense the reaction will be in the future because we are healing that part of ourselves.

Book Recommendations

- *The Relentless Courage Of A Sacred Child* – Tana Amen

Notes

- Attune to your inner child. Listen to the triggers that come up. Those triggers become our roadmap in returning to ourselves and meeting the emotional wounds of our past with a more present, grown up version of ourselves.

- In being in tune with our inner child and our body's emotions, our bodies no longer have to carry the weight of the past, holding on to what we were not ready to face, and instead, our bodies get to let go and breathe.

- Inner-child dialogue – "I see you (insert name here), what are you feeling?

Vocalize: Breaking a spirit of fear

"The cave you fear to enter holds the treasure you seek." – Joseph Campbell

Healing isn't linear, yet it slowly connects with each layer we pull back. We've seen the emotional side, the physical side, and pieces of the mental side. That leaves us with the spiritual side. As someone who defines themselves as a spiritual person, believing in God, I became familiar with the term "spiritual warfare" as I began to hear it more often.

I learned what I was experiencing was shared among others. Those seasons of anxiety, panic attacks, and extreme nausea led me to more and more individuals who had a similar story. It became less frightening to know I was not alone in what I was going through. Through spiritual eyes, I began to hear the now common words "spirit of fear" and how it was connected to my symptoms.

Fear is often talked about in terms of "facing your fears" in an external sense, yet there is also this embedded internal fear that has shaped our way of living and being. That is the fear I am going to address here. The fear that has made you live in a box, constantly asking, "What if that could happen?" or "I can't do that because of..." You can fill in the blank. A fear that keeps you from trusting yourself and those around you. A spirit of fear consumes you and stops you from living in a place of safety but instead pushes you to operate from a sense of constant threat.

Addressing Fear's Residence — *Roommate Dream*

It's morning and I am sitting on the couch as my roommate comes in to sit next to me. "I had a dream about you last night," she says as I wait, somewhat excited yet a little cautious. "Here's the dream. You came home after hanging out with a guy, what seemed like just a hangout, and started to tell me about it. As you were telling me about it, your body starts to shake, and then your whole body starts convulsing. At that point, I start to pray and specifically pray about a spirit of fear." I sit there, hoping that would never happen in real life and pondering what that meant for me.

What I thought was normal behavior was actually fear. With each layer, I connected the dots. Intense anxiety in dating, the onset of nausea the closer I got to intimacy, and the themes of sexual, verbal, and physical abuse were all in my family history, along with the physical passing down of trauma and learned experiences. There was an additional layer—the spiritual side.

I began to approach my fear surrounding getting close to men. I went from a past of growing up only feeling comfortable with my brothers, having one guy friend in kindergarten (which almost held me back), to keeping men as acquaintances as I healed. Through dating and each intentional male friendship, I saw myself gradually walking through a fear that originally branded itself into my identity. I learned to live a life as Cassie, no longer connected to that fear, that "security" from what I thought to be a threat. As I approached the heaviest layers, I knew I already survived the hardest part—it was now just getting to its end.

Changing The Narrative — *Dance Event*

OK Cassie, if you see him tonight, just ask. Just do it, I try to calmly say to myself.

This was a little bit of my pep talk before running into a guy I have a little crush on but really want to build more of a friendship with. There I am, standing around the usual people I see on this weeknight when he comes by. When I see him, my body immediately responds, almost like having butterflies but in fast-forward motion.

Cassie, you got this. Breathe.

He comes up to me, and we chit-chat a little, and then, here I go. I have rehearsed this line over and over to prepare myself, which goes a little like, "Let's keep the birthday celebration going. Can I get you a belated birthday drink?" However, it doesn't always go as planned. My response was, "I'd love to treat you to a birthday drink." Much more formal and direct yet still appropriate. After that statement, immediately nausea floods my body. Not just butterflies—it was like a tidal wave of anxiety and nausea all in one. As I walk away, I start to process.

Is this a sign that this isn't a good choice? Will I ever be able to date if this is what it is going to feel like? Is this feeling ever going to end?

I am in my thoughts and suddenly, another comes—one I have not heard before. *It's time to approach it differently, stand up to the fear, and walk through it.* Another comes right after. *We are not going to live like this anymore. We are going to fucking move through it.* Immediately, with that thinking in mind, the feeling dissipates. I start to recognize this piece of the journey is spiritual.

There were two differences that night. First, I was aware of what was taking place in my body. Second, I believed it would be different. I was able to commit to myself, knowing that my body and I would make it through. That night taught me that nausea may not be over, but the more I walked through those triggers, the less they would have a hold on me. In a spiritual sense, the less room the spirit of fear had to reside in me, the more peace was allowed to take its place.

"Cassie, God uses some people to take out this pocket of pain in our lives," I remembered my counselor saying to reassure me. I knew my previous relationship opened my eyes to be aware of the pain my body carried, and now I was being invited to let my body pour out the weight of it. This is the real journey. Take this same guy as an example.

I could have kept telling myself, "This guy is toxic. He is triggering me." Yes, there is truth to that, but sometimes people bring out needed areas of healing in our lives. The beautiful part is seeing your own progression. I got to see that for myself with this gentleman.

At the beginning of meeting him, I would feel a constant fear and un-easiness, but as months passed, that fear slowly dissipated, and I saw more and more groundedness within myself and confidence in my own voice. Before, the anxiety I experienced in my body was from the belief that I didn't have a voice or a choice around men, but the more I walked through the small steps of building a friendship with this man in particular, I slowly healed some of those triggers as my voice and sense of control came back to me.

The more we become aware of something, the less fear has a hold on our bodies and minds. When I discovered that this was also a spiritual battle, I knew better how to address it and how to respond. Even knowing what was happening in my brain and being aware that my subconscious was at play, I had a greater grace for myself and greater hope in knowing that my awareness would calm any sense of panic.

In facing fear, we discover how strong our voice really is and how much fear has taken from us. Our voice is our sword—it is our way to reclaim the ground that was taken from us through life circumstances, trauma, and pain. It's in moments like the one I shared above that we discover how pivotal our voices are and their significance in our healing.

Gaining Spiritual Awareness — *Blood Work — Lazarus Season Conclusion*

"This is some of the best blood work I've seen." My body sighs in relief while I am still hoping to gain some answers. I am coming off a three-day series of panic attacks, little food, and constant anxiousness, thinking this must be more than my mind. While I am pressing into the medical side of things, I realize the spiritual side needs my attention if my blood work indicates my health is fine. So, I lean in the direction of taking my energy to the spiritual side of things.

I start with finding practical ways to confront fear, anxiety, and worry on a daily basis. I read books, articles, and podcasts. Anything to inform me on what I am experiencing. I guard my mornings with declarations of peace over my mind and body, and I begin to speak my healing into existence. I have many mornings where I think, "This isn't working" or "This is pointless," but I keep saying to myself, "It will break, it has to." I mean, I don't really have another option. I can choose negative thinking, but I know I will stay in the same physical state.

I had to make a choice. A choice to believe my physical state would change. As I chose to continue to participate in regular activities like dance training, going outside, and meeting with people, I chose to not give anxiety or fear a permanent place in my life. Even in what felt like torment, I continued to hold onto the idea that it would break off me. Not that I would never experience it again, but I would have a strategy as to how to approach it and that I would never experience it to this degree.

I believe that our wounding opens us up to the enemy to create a hold in our lives. For me, that was fear. Sometimes that wounding happens so young we are unaware of that hold because it becomes a habit with how we live. For me, I lived with fear for so long that I believed it was part of my personality. It's not. Absolutely not.

When we get to a place where our body is ready to address some wounds, all the trash, all the pain surfaces. What got me through was staying in the community, continuing my process with my counselor, speaking declarations in the morning, and, throughout the day, doing "fun" things that reminded me, "This too shall pass."

Over time, the grip of fear loosened and I learned how strong my body and myself were. Still, to this day, I may wake up feeling anxious or nauseous, but now I have a rhythm. I journal, I stretch, I do breathing exercises, and if I still feel something in my body, I converse with my body and stay aware throughout the day. Instead of starting to panic, I choose to partner with my body, trusting it will show me what it needs.

Understanding Unconscious Fear — *Personal Study*

A big part of my journey was understanding how and why my body would react before I could trace a thought or a memory. In my pursuit to know and understand my body, I found *Life Unlocked, 7 Revolutionary Lessons to Overcome Fear* by Srinivasan S. Pillay M.D.

It all started with this sentence: "Fear can easily register in the amygdala without being passed on to the cortex, preventing you from knowing that you have been exposed to something fearful. To have an emotional response, you do not have to know about the fear; it only needs to be registered by the unconscious brain." (Srinivasan, S. Pillay, *Life Unlocked: 7 Revolutionary Lessons To Overcome Fear.* Rodale Inc, 2010, pp. 11.)

Here I will share a story from the book to paint a picture of how fear shows up in the body and how this might show up in someone's life. A man in a corporate position, let's name him Jamal, had a steady job. However, he was slowly beginning to resent his position, yet was too afraid to step out as an entrepreneur. He began seeing Dr. Pillay after suffering from recurring panic attacks without warning of their onset. In the internal turmoil, there were contradictory messages being sent to the "action center" or motor cortex of his brain. One message saying, "Let's move on and get this done," and another saying, "Don't do this. You're in danger."

"Panic attacks are associated with increased amygdala activation that likely disrupts the functioning of the cortex and, in particular, of the part called the anterior cingulate cortex (ACC). From a neurological perspective, whenever Brian's cortex tried to move him toward his goal, the riptide generated by his overactive amygdala disrupted his cortical intentions, dragging him further away." (Srinivasan, S. Pillay, *Life Unlocked: 7 Revolutionary Lessons To Overcome Fear.* Rodale Inc, 2010, pp. 13.)

Fear was invisible to the man who was walking through the internal chaos, yet it brought clarity to my own journey to break past the fear of men.

"Hope is not an answer. Rather as something that stimulates the imagination, hope helps us to pose the right questions, just as a hypothesis helps a scientist design experiments." Motor Maps are "action plans based on information that we give the brain. They are highly dependent on what we imagine. If we remain fearful, fear will disrupt our imagination. If we focus on our goals instead of 'the fear,' the brain can use what we imagine as a guide for sketching out a motor map." (Srinivasan, S. Pillay, *Life Unlocked: 7 Revolutionary Lessons To Overcome Fear.* Rodale Inc, 2010, pp. 51.)

The next step is shifting from a fear focus to a goal/objective focus. Finding ourselves and our voice starts with finding where it's been suffocated by fear and then moving through that barrier. As we journey in reclaiming and standing in our voice, I believe simultaneously we reclaim part of our bodies.

We are choosing to champion ourselves and, therefore, pour value back into ourselves that was stolen by fear. There are tools to guide us, and as we face spiritual resistance, I believe we will see abundance as we push back and uncover the voice that has always been within us. What might feel like a barrier may be a setup for us to see the lion that is already within us.

Reflection

- Have you ever heard the term "spirit of fear?" What are your thoughts around it? Have you experienced something similar in your life?

- How have you seen fear show up in your relationship with people and in your relationship with yourself?

- What have been helpful tools in helping you face and address any fear in your life?

Next Steps

- Take some time to journal and respond to the questions above. The more we become aware of fear and how it shows up in our lives the more authority we carry in knowing we are still in control of our minds and our bodies. Take a look at a few books to gain a deeper understanding of the spiritual side of fear.

Resources

- *Life Unlocked, 7 Revolutionary Lessons to Overcome Fear* – Srinivasan S. Pillay M.D

- *Spirit Wars* – Kris Vallotton

  ○ Addressing the spirit of fear and staying free

- *Tools for Breakthrough* – Shaun Bolz

  ○ Declarations, prayers, and scripture on specific areas of needed healing

Notes

- A spirit of fear inhibits us from living in a place of safety and instead pushes us to operate from a sense of constant threat.

- The more we become aware of something the less fear has a hold on our body and our mind.

- Our voice is our sword. It is our way to reclaim the ground that was taken from us through life's circumstances, trauma, and pain.

- Finding your voice starts with finding where it's been suppressed. In what experiences, what memories and in what areas has it been suffocated? As we journey in reclaiming and standing in our voice, I believe simultaneously we reclaim part of our bodies.

Progression: Walking out your healing

"This is the day that everything can change for you." – Michael S. Hyatt

As I shared earlier, I am not a therapist, even though I've had many people mistake me for one. I am not certified, and I do not have credentials; I have my story. If you need healing and freedom from the places I've been, my story and this book are for you. The stories of other women rescued me as a form of provision, delivering me from the pain I carried in my body. You are meant to live whole, and you are meant to live full.

"*Si cambio, yo cambio el mundo*/I change myself, I change the world." (Gloria Anzaldúa)

Now, what does that look like to live together with our bodies? It is the decision to continue to choose to commit to our bodies, to our healing and to strengthening our friendship with ourselves.

As I look back now, the way I made it through was by being forced to make a choice. Am I going to continue to choose fear and panic or make a decision in my mind that I will make it through and choose to believe something different; a mindset altered by my belief, a mindset of faith.

As you live forward with your body, it is an adventure, with highs and lows, but the main objective is a deeper connection. With that commitment in mind, watch as you see your life shift and unfold like nothing before.

Exposure Therapy — *Next Level Conference*

"Group 13, come to the front." My girlfriends and I are at this conference called Next Level Experience. We have no idea what to expect, but we know we are here for something that will leave us with a different approach to life. As I walk to the front of the stage to see who else is in my group, I realize my group is all men.

"Well, look at that. Our first group of all men with one woman," the conference speaker states.

I am so over this, I think to myself. *Well, we are going to have to just do this, so let's do it, Cassie.*

It's time to test out how comfortable I feel with my body and recognize my progress. As I make my way near my group, I see my girlfriends in the corner giving me the eye. I know in their heads they are saying, "*God totally set this up.*"

Now part of the healing journey isn't so much that I experience that panic or fear from before, but now it is the exposure therapy of being more comfortable around men. That comfort first comes with trusting and finding security in myself.

With moments like this, of getting more exposure around men, any lingering fear left in my body and mind will slowly have to go. Less fear with more exposure. As I build trust in myself, the confidence I carry comes with a greater foundation, allowing me to approach life from a sense of power over powerlessness.

There comes a time when you can no longer move forward with the same way of living. It's as if life is forcing you to change. More experiences like the one above continued to happen as if life was asking me, *How are you going to choose to continue to live*? How I spoke, how I behaved around men, and the lack of trust in myself kept me living a certain way.

It kept me in a bubble. A bubble that said, "I can only live like this to stay safe." That bubble wouldn't serve me in the long run. To address it, I started with how I spoke.

I noticed my language kept giving space and power to men who were no longer in my life. Their actions still had a hold on me. I could choose to partner with my past and continue to let my experiences identify me, or I could decide to identify with who I am without the baggage. What that looked like for me was a lot of internal self-talk, movement-focused therapy, and reading narratives of those who have experienced something similar.

For the vast majority of my life, I was comfortable with hiding and being in situations that had no men involved, which started to show no benefits in regard to work and opportunities. There came a time when I had to no longer be comfortable in my pain, but make the decision to work through it to get to the other side, and really reconnect with me.

Even though I didn't know how to see myself in a new light, there came a point where my language went from, "I have been through this, and this is why I am like this," to, "Even though this is my experience, it does not hold weight in who I am now." I'm not saying to not validate what we have experienced, but I decided I wouldn't just stop there. I would name my experience but no longer let it hold power over my life and name me. I saw as my intentions shifted, my language shifted, and my body released that stagnant energy, and eventually, different men came into my life.

With each layer, different men entered my life. This allowed me to face whatever pain and residue that still remained in my body. I was learning how to build healthy friendships with men and how to heal the pain I identified with for so long. I used to hear it all the time that it's easier not to change because it can be less painful, but the pain of not changing can make someone reconsider.

For me, when more men entered my life, it felt threatening at first, especially once they passed the acquaintance level. That showed me how long I had lived keeping a wall from healthy connection. Having spent years letting that wall down, I can say the other side has so much more to offer that I didn't trust at first.

I even used to say, "I prefer to be single because I know it will be more comfortable and safer for me." It is not easy. It does take time and courage to first face our story and then to walk through it. The beauty lies in the moments where we can reconnect with ourselves and open ourselves up to even richer connections with other human beings.

The First Encounter — *Choreography Project*

"There will be physical contact in this dance piece, but no sexual touching. What are you comfortable with and what are you not comfortable with?" my friend Jaja, the choreographer, asks.

Cassie, you can do this, and it's your friend. She knows you and knows how to create a safe space. I start to list out any minor fears that creep in. Other choreography projects have been presented to me in the past, but I turned them down for the sake of what felt safe to me. *I think it will be different this time,* I say to myself with a sense of grounded assurance. I decide to jump in, believing I can do what my friend is envisioning. Our first rehearsal was my test.

"Cassie, I want you to lay your body over his shoulder and completely relax. Let him carry your weight," Jaja instructs. I sense a hesitancy in myself, yet it's met with a grounded calmness. Without much resistance I let my body go as I press into trusting this man, a somewhat known acquaintance. "From there, I want you to stand close to each other and look one another in the eye for a sense of momentary connection."

I can really do this, I reassure myself. My eyes move from the ground up as I meet his gaze. I notice I don't feel afraid, my body isn't shaking, and I feel calm. I feel empowered almost. *I'm in control now*, I say to myself as a smirk crescents upon my face.

I really did that. I really did that. It took me some time to get here, but this is what it feels like to be healthy, be mature, and be free, I debrief in my head.

Throughout the rehearsals and the duration of the project, I received invites to other forms of contact that would test the comfort I felt in my body, with myself and with another man. I walked away from those rehearsals seeing the benefits of taking my time in walking through my healing. I got to see my progress, reflecting on the idea that if this opportunity had been presented to me years prior, I do not think it would have been safe or even possible for me.

The beautiful part is seeing moments like these where you can say to yourself, "Look how far you have come—you wouldn't have been able to do this a year ago." Learn to celebrate the little wins because you can look back and see they were huge in those moments. Those wins brought you to where you are now.

As you keep moving forward, here are a few tools I continue to use in moving forward with healing and living more present in my body.

Taking Body Inventory

I can do it, and this is fun, I scream a little on the inside. Music is blasting as I see a man approach me. It is all in slow motion as I listen to the tape in my head. *It's OK. Just try it out and remember you are in control. You are in control!* I see him reach out his hand, inviting me to join him on the dance floor. In a sea of people moving in different directions, I slowly join in.

This is a salsa club, and partner dancing is the essence of this place. I say to myself, *Cassie, look at that. You are doing it.* I feel a sense of empowerment and comfort as I choose to dance with this stranger. Tonight, I am choosing not to hesitate and go for it, reminding myself I am in control.

A year ago, I came to the same club, literally denying every guy who asked to dance with me out of complete fear. My body was as hard as a statue, destined to not move from the place I was sitting. The salsa club was my self-inventory homework, letting me see where I was in feeling comfortable with my body and around men.

Self-Inventory

Being in situations that may have felt triggering before and now recognizing the difference. Checking in with our bodies, seeing what isn't there that may have been there before. Seeing how some triggers may have dissipated and where fear no longer lingers. Debriefing with ourselves to see if there is growth and healing has sunk in. Exposing ourselves slowly to places that once felt threatening and now we feel empowered in.

Self-Inventory Questions:

* What do I feel in my body? Is this a similar reaction or feeling from before?

* Where do I see growth? Where do I see a similar reaction or feeling? Or a different one?

* How can I acknowledge where I am showing up differently and how my body is feeling more secure?

Self-Talk

"What is your concrete self-talk?" I am sitting in the car quietly as my body slumps into the seat. Feeling partially defeated, my head lays back on the headrest behind me. "Will this ever end? Can I just be like the other girls? Can my healing just come in one moment and not be this gradual, constant thing to work on? Why do I have to deal with this? I didn't ask for it, and I don't want it."

That is my ongoing tape. My counselor is hearing me share another moment where I have been feeling nausea in my body after being invited to hang out with a guy. I have gone through months walking out of the depth of my pain and feel I am 75% on the other side. However, I notice in situations of hanging out with men one-on-one, I still have subtle anxiety that keeps me feeling full with no appetite. I know my techniques, I know the thoughts to place in my head, and I am just getting tired at times of doing the work and wanting to just be carried. I want it to be over.

"No, Cassie, you are breaking the pattern, and it is almost over," she says. "You are at the end of it."

"I can say I did notice something different this time. When I feel nauseous, I start with taking deep breaths and saying, 'It's going to be OK, and this feeling is going to pass,' and I actually feel the nausea leave." That is the self-talk she is referring to. It's the process of breaking a pattern your body is choosing in order to keep itself in control and in feeling "safe."

In the moments when I felt nauseated, I chose to reach out to my counselor or friend, who journeyed with me from the beginning. She focused my attention on what to celebrate and how far I had come. Second, she showed me how to recognize the onset of nausea—subtle anxiety or stomach tightening. That was my body's way of warning me that it was overwhelmed or feeling stressed. She invited me to begin asking myself, "What does my heart need, and what do I need to listen to?"

Her questions taught me to be attentive to the beginning signs of my body reacting and attend to my body before it went into a downward spiral. "It's in the discipline of self-talk and the techniques that will break this pattern that has been in your life and even generationally for years," my counselor wisely left me with.

Sometimes when we feel even a small amount of the same pain we've already walked through, we may be tempted to think we've gone backward. In reality, it's the residue that's left that gets washed out because we've survived the hardest part. On the days when we continue to experience the residue, we can invite friends to pray, to communicate, and to walk alongside us. Even when it feels like the healing journey is overwhelming, it's important to have people around us who can speak right into the situation, trusting that freedom will come even when we feel too tired to endure.

Examine your self-talk narrative. I realized that nausea, fear, and anxiety were not just going to go away. I really had to walk through it. Meaning I would have to do some exposure therapy of hanging out with men more often to move past the fear that had held me back for so many years, and in doing so, I had to talk myself through it.

In moving forward, it's listening to our bodies, doing the self-talk homework and going through it, one experience at a time. Here are some self-talk takeaways:

"I got through this before, I can get through it again."

"It's not that big of a deal; look at how it went last time. I felt good after."

"It's going to be OK."

It is a big deal—what your body is experiencing. So, with self-talk, it helped me refocus and say, "It's going to get better."

Repeat these lines multiple times if needed. You can repeat it aloud or in your mind and take constant deep breaths to reset your body when you feel overwhelmed. Somedays you may find yourself saying these every hour or every fifteen minutes. It's in building a new paradigm shift and doing the "homework" as my counselor would say. We may be tempted by the idea of a magic button for all the pain or fear to dissipate, but sometimes freedom is gradual, regaining the territory, step by step.

Self-Trust

The internal work continued while I was simultaneously met with surprising moments of progress. There were the seasons of releasing the fear from my body and then the invitation to build a new structure from within.

From this moment where I had the opportunity to do a creative project with this gentleman, I was launched into a season of working primarily with men. More opportunities working with men came into my path which revealed areas of my growth and areas where more healing was coming. These interactions were showing me I was closer to letting men back into my life while the control was now in my hands.

Looking back, the months of intense nausea, panic attacks, and years of ingrained fear had lost its power over my life. I saw a new version of me emerge. A me that came out of hiding, a me that even surprised myself in these different situations. Still having moments of anxious thought cycles and slight nervousness, a grounded trust in myself and a sense of security within my own body yet came forth.

Within one year, all this transpired. I started working on dance projects with men, started dating again without minimal body reactions, and I attended a wedding where I faced a person who embodied a lot of my unforgiveness and pain. My dad.

It was like God knew this was the time. The time to face the final layers of fear and I now had the tools and trust with myself to walk me through.

This was my reminder, and I say the same encouragement to you, that even though it feels like it can take forever to heal, to release the past, to be free, there is healing that isn't always visible at first. Something is happening in our obedience to stay disciplined to care for ourselves. It's in the little steps, the little shifts, and in continuously choosing to still show up. There will be those surprise moments where you get to say, "Wow, I did that," from, "I couldn't have imagined doing or saying that a year ago."

The you that has always been there is emerging; it's the shedding off of fear, generational pain and trauma, to uncover the beauty of you that was never meant to be hidden. Healing is forever a process, yet we move into deeper layers of self-trust giving us the tools of how to face what is to come next.

Imagining What Is Ahead

"I am free of this. I am traveling and teaching others how to be free. I no longer experience nausea around men. I have a partner and am not afraid of connection." I take a deep breath as my body relaxes, acknowledging what I am saying is one day going to be true. Another tool my counselor shared is future-oriented.

Imagining myself in ten years, where will I be? Speaking what is ahead into the present, trusting this isn't permanent but temporary. It makes the current feeling and heaviness feel approachable and bearable because I know and am speaking my way through it to the other side.

Imagine. Write out those few statements of where you will be in ten years. Free. You will look back and think, I remember that season and what it taught me, and look where I am now.

Reflection
- As you hear the different tools mentioned: Body Inventory, Self-Talk, & Imagining ahead, what seems most accessible/relatable to you?

- Have you used some of these tools already and how have they aided you in building reconnection with your body and self?

Next Steps
- Choose a tool. For the next month, commit to trying that tool twice a week. As you partner with the tool you choose, write down any thoughts or feelings that start to arise. A deeper sense of self-awareness and body connection? Feeling a sense of separation or barriers? In spending more time tuning into your process, see what the tool brings you.

Notes
- As you live forward with your body, it is an adventure with highs and lows, but the main objective is a deeper connection.

Celebration: Cultivating an atmosphere of love

"You are a sea of light, open your eyes and see yourself." – Nayyirah Waheed

I want to leave us with this. Celebrate all the way. Daily. Momentarily. When we choose to celebrate, the negativity has less room, less of a hold. Our focus shifts, and we begin to notice more moments to celebrate. We are pouring into a cup of gratitude and that gratitude will shift our perspective and affect how we are living life. When we celebrate, we also pour into the cup of hope, believing and holding onto what is coming but is not yet. Celebrating reminds us to stay present and accept where we are in the moment while looking at how far we have come.

I disciplined myself in celebrating my progress with little daily exercises. For example, in my journal, I would write "Progress or Highlights," and I would remind myself daily, when possible, of the things I was proud of myself for and the progress I would see. Someone once told me, "Embrace your movement, embrace yourself, embrace where you are right now," and watch what will open up. Our lives will evolve in an authentic way when we choose ourselves and choose to embrace where we are.

In creating an attitude of celebration, my dance training, my perspective toward life, and my self-talk all mirrored a sense of grace and confidence that wasn't there before. That confidence grew steadily in other areas of my life as a product of the work I chose in cultivating how to celebrate myself.

We may want the healing, the results to come faster, or to be further ahead. Those "wants" that create a craving to be somewhere else rather than where we are, keep us from experiencing the rich moment we are presently in. Celebration keeps us rooted in the present. When we shift our focus on where we see progress, we begin to see more progress versus focusing on lack and only starting to see lack.

As we choose to take on an attitude of celebration, I trust we will see our progress blossom before our eyes.

Let's celebrate our growth, let's celebrate our stories. May we be encouraged through the journey and may we remember how valuable we all are.

Reflection

- When you hear the word "celebration," what comes to mind?

- How have you celebrated yourself in the past? How may that look similar or different now?

- Where can you start to implement a discipline of celebration?

Next Steps

Start right now.

What can you celebrate today?

How have you seen yourself grow, and what are you proud of yourself for? Where have you seen yourself show up that you want to acknowledge? You are worth being celebrated.

Notes

- Celebrating reminds us to stay present and accept where we are in the moment while looking at how far we have come.

- Our life will evolve in an authentic way when we choose ourselves and choose to embrace where we are at.

- Celebration keeps us rooted in the present.

The End

"Our experiences shape us, even the painful ones, and how you overcome them is how you bless the world with your story." – Cassandra Tsolis

The depths of our story find us even when we may not want them to. With each season of unfolding, there comes a deeper awareness of what is within us and what lies ahead. Even though we don't see it all right away, there is intention in how we were made and what we were made for.

I was sitting in a coffee shop contemplating what I thought about God after listening to a sermon with this line repeating in my head, "God has chosen his people." Slightly frustrated leaving the service, I asked my friend to drop me off at a coffee shop as we left.

Sitting in silence, I put my bible out on the table in front of me and started making faces as I sarcastically barked, "How do I know if God chose me?" I didn't really know what to think and I didn't really want to read but I decided to. I opened up my bible in hopes to find an answer to that question that haunted my mind.

"Can I sit with you?" My eyes timidly looked up to see a middle-aged woman approaching, looking as if she was going to sit down. "I see you have a bible. Do you believe in God?"

Still hardly speaking at this point, I nodded and finally got some words out of my mouth, accepting her invitation to sit. I spent the next twenty to thirty minutes hearing her story of how God had healed her of an illness, how God met her in a personal way, and what was happening in her life now.

"Have you ever heard of prophecy or an encouraging word?" she asked. I shook my head as I noticed butterflies arise in my stomach, uncertain of what she was about to say. "I felt like God invited me to come to this coffee shop, and when I came in, you were highlighted to me. God wants me to tell you that he has chosen you. He has chosen you and He is going to use you to heal other women and encourage other women in their identity."

Freeze. Everything went in slow motion around me. I started to look around, thinking I was not in this world. I wanted to scream. I wanted to jump around; all this energy was exploding within my body. Moments later, she left, and immediately I called my friend.

"You won't believe what just happened to me."

When my friend came to pick me up, I was finally screaming, not believing what just happened. That moment marked my life. I had known that prophecy was a way that God made himself personal to people and that day, I knew there was more to God and that God saw me. What I didn't know was what the rest of my story held and what it really meant to bring women into healing as I first had to face the healing in my own story.

That moment happened nine years ago. I believe what that woman spoke over me is what I am living out now. We walk through our own stories before we can walk with others through theirs.

Through my journey, this is where the birth of Echo Movement, a small business I started in 2022, began. A space intended to aid individuals in listening to the wisdom of their body through therapeutic tools and movement prompts. The tools, insight, and research I learned through my own adventure back to self, I infused into this program, and I want to also offer you. If this book brought a sense of clarity and relief to you, I invite you to partake in Echo Movement. You can participate and learn more at www.cassandratsolis.com/workshops-private-sessions and @echomovementsessions.

Remember, we need your story. Your story will set someone else free, just as my friend's story did for me. Your body has been your advocate all this time. It's been waiting to talk with you, live in union with you, and approach life together. There is no greater bond than the one you have with your body. It's time to come home to you.

References

Chapter 2

- Goggin, Caitlyn. "The Efficacy of Dance/Movement Therapy for Trauma Affected Youth." *Lesley University*, 19 May 2018, https://digitalcommons.lesley.edu/expressive_theses/93/.

- Gregory, Amanda Ann. "How Bottom-Up Treatment Can Address Trauma. *Psychology Today*, 19 Dec. 2021, https://www.psychologytoday.com/us/blog/simplifying-complex-trauma/202112/how-bottom-treatment-can-address-trauma.

- Wolynn, Mark. *It Didn't Start with You: How Inherited Family Trauma Shapes Who We Are and How to End the Cycle.* Penguin Books, 2017.

Chapter 3

- Wolynn, Mark. *It Didn't Start with You: How Inherited Family Trauma Shapes Who We Are and How to End the Cycle.* Penguin Books, 2017.

- Levine, Peter. *Waking the Tiger*, North Atlantic Books 1997.

Chapter 4

- Wolynn, Mark. *It Didn't Start with You: How Inherited Family Trauma Shapes Who We Are and How to End the Cycle*. Penguin Books, 2017.

- Van der Kolk, Bessel. *The Body Keeps the Score: Brain, Mind, and Body in the Healing of Trauma*. Penguin Books, 2014.

Chapter 5

- Wolynn, Mark. *It Didn't Start with You: How Inherited Family Trauma Shapes Who We Are and How to End the Cycle*. Penguin Books, 2017.

- Van der Kolk, Bessel. *The Body Keeps the Score: Brain, Mind, and Body in the Healing of Trauma*. Penguin Books, 2014.

Chapter 6

- Wolynn, Mark. *It Didn't Start with You: How Inherited Family Trauma Shapes Who We Are and How to End the Cycle*. Penguin Books, 2017.

Chapter 7

- Heshmat, Shahram. "What Is the Dissociative Mind?" *Psychology Today*, 10 Feb. 2021, www.psychologytoday.com/us/blog/science-of-choice/202102/what-is-the-dissociative-mind.

- "Self-Hatred." *Psychology Today*, www.psychologytoday.com/us/basics/self-hatred.

Chapter 10

- Srinivasan, S. Pillay, *Life Unlocked: 7 Revolutionary Lessons To Overcome Fear.* Rodale Inc, 2010.

Made in the USA
Las Vegas, NV
07 December 2024

13543968R00080